Children's
FURNITURE
projects

Children's FURNITURE *projects*

With Step-by-Step Instructions and Complete Plans

JEFF MILLER

The Taunton Press

The Taunton Press
Inspiration for hands-on living™

The Taunton Press, Inc., 63 South Main Street, PO Box 5506, Newtown, CT 06470-5506
e-mail: tp@taunton.com

Distributed by Publishers Group West

EDITOR: Rick Mastelli
COVER DESIGN: Ann Marie Manca
INTERIOR DESIGN: Lori Wendin
LAYOUT: Suzie Yannes
ILLUSTRATOR: Melanie Powell
PHOTOGRAPHER: Tanya Tucka

LIBRARY OF CONGRESS CATALOGING-IN-PUBLICATION DATA:
Miller, Jeff, 1956–
    Children's furniture projects : with step-by-step instructions and
complete plans / author, Jeff Miller ; photographer, Tanya Tucka.
        p. cm.
    ISBN 1-56158-504-1
    1. Children's furniture. I. Title.
    TT197.5 .C5 M55 2002
    684.1--dc21   2002004329

WORKING WITH WOOD IS INHERENTLY DANGEROUS. Using hand or power tools improperly or ignoring safety practices can lead to permanent injury or even death. Don't try to perform operations you learn about here (or elsewhere) unless you're certain they are safe for you. If something about an operation doesn't feel right, don't do it. Look for another way. We want you to enjoy the craft, so please keep safety foremost in your mind whenever you're in the shop.

Printed in the United States of America
10 9 8 7 6 5 4 3 2 1

To Isaac and Ariel

ACKNOWLEDGMENTS

BY THE TIME A BOOK LIKE THIS is finished, many people will have given support in many different ways. I value the help I have received in the shop from Jason Holtz, Alice Tacheny, Eyal Goldblatt, and Andy Brownell. Tanya Tucka takes great photographs and is a delight to work with, book after book. And Tom Clark and Rick Mastelli with Taunton helped keep me on target.

I am especially grateful to Jane Stenson and her kindergarten students for allowing me to come into their classroom, where they easily matched my enthusiasm for children's chairs with their own creativity, excitement, and energy.

And thanks always to Becky.

CONTENTS

INTRODUCTION

My first experience with making furniture for a child came when my niece (the first child in her generation of my family) turned two and I wanted to make something special for her birthday. There was an awful lot I didn't know about children then, and the results of my efforts didn't turn out exactly as I intended. Fortunately, things weren't a total disaster. My niece quickly grew big enough to use the piece I made for her.

I decided I needed to learn a little more. Over the years, not only have I done more research on making furniture for children but I have also had many other occasions to learn from my mistakes. I've learned even more from the children around me, and especially from my own. It has always been both fun and rewarding.

The main thing I have discovered is that making furniture for children is not quite the same as making furniture for adults. Kids use stuff differently, and they have different needs, desires, and tastes. That's not to say that most of the things we pay attention to when making adult furniture don't apply. On the contrary. We still have to work toward good design, appropriate structure and construction, and proper finishing. But most of the requirements are a bit different from what we look for in our grown-up work.

Good design for children involves a number of factors. First and foremost is safety. Furniture, especially for infants and younger children, must be as safe as we can make it. Many of the safety issues are not entirely obvious, especially if you don't have much experience with children already. Fortunately, there are plenty of guidelines to help us with this, and they are discussed in Children's Furniture Basics (p. 4). Safety is also a factor when choosing methods of construction and finishing. This furniture needs to stand up to all of the stresses and indignities a child will dish out, and it must be safe even if chewed on.

Once all of this is out of the way, we come to making things that are special for children. There are many ways to approach this, and many of these approaches can be combined. One possibility is to make a child-size version of a piece of grown-up furniture. A child feels special having his or her own version of something that adults commonly use. The miniature Four-Poster Bed (p. 48) is a great example of this.

Another possibility is to make something that is uniquely for kids. After speaking with a group of kindergarteners about chairs, I discovered that they liked the idea of a chair that was also something else—something more than just a chair. This is not a grown-up concept. And that makes pieces like the Marble Chair (p. 106) very special, something kids have a hard time resisting.

Children's furniture can also be designed with an element of whimsy: the Child's Rocker (p. 90) and the Toy Chest (p. 138) fit in with this. There are geometric shapes, patterns, and colors to play with. And there are pieces that tie in with strong childhood interests, like the Rocking Dinosaur (p. 124). And finally, there are pieces that just plain function well for children, such as the Versatile Children's Table (p. 78).

The designs in this book are for real furniture for real kids. Some of it is playful; some of it is like Mom's and Dad's; but all of it is useful, fun, durable, and something children and parents—and especially the person who made it—will be proud of. Each of the projects can be used as a simple set of plans for a high-quality project, a starting point for variations, or even the foundation for a project of your own design.

Many of these designs evolved from things I made for my own children and thus have been field-tested extensively by them, by my nieces and nephews, and by the children of many customers who have purchased children's furniture from me over the course of my career as a furniture designer and craftsman.

I hope you enjoy them as much as we have.

CHILDREN'S
FURNITURE BASICS

BEFORE YOU PROCEED headlong into
building furniture for children, it is
helpful to learn more about some of
the topics that are specific to this kind
of furniture. The main issue, of course, is safety,
and this pervades many of the discussions—
whether they be about design, construction,
or finish. In the broad sense, that is what this
chapter is about. But there are also issues of
sizing, and you'll find some jigs to help with
some of the basics of construction.

Safety Standards

Commercially manufactured furniture for
children and especially that for infants must
adhere to some fairly specific guidelines.
Most of these come from the U.S. Consumer
Product Safety Commission (CPSC) and the
American Society for Testing and Materials
(ASTM), which look at data on injuries and
deaths from a wide range of products and
then try to determine causes for the accidents. These organizations also devise tests

SAFETY RESOURCES

If you would like more complete safety information on children's
furniture or on a huge variety of other subjects, contact the following
organizations:

U.S. Consumer Product
   Safety Commission
Washington, DC 20207
Hotline: 800-638-2772
Web site: www.cpsc.gov

American Society for Testing
   and Materials
100 Barr Harbor Drive
West Conshohocken, PA 19428
Phone: 610-832-9585
Web site: www.astm.org

Crib Safety: The Posts

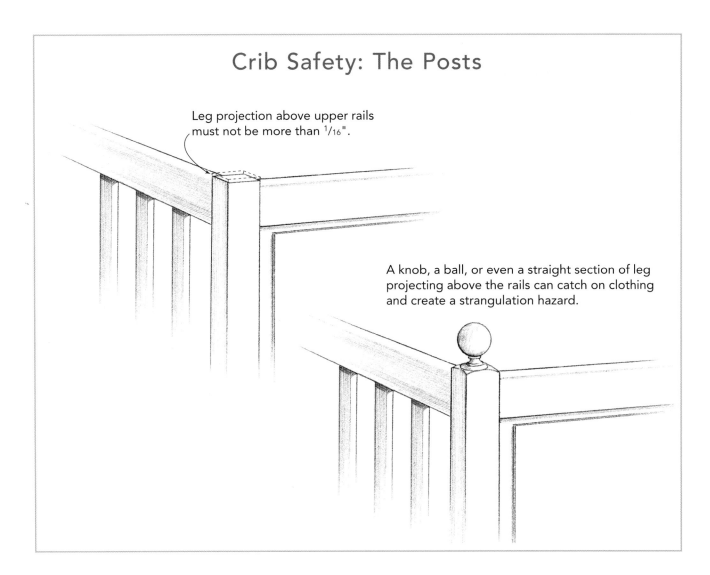

Leg projection above upper rails must not be more than $^{1}/_{16}$".

A knob, a ball, or even a straight section of leg projecting above the rails can catch on clothing and create a strangulation hazard.

to simulate some of the problems that led to the accidents and ultimately come up with safety standards or recommendations. Each is a good resource when looking to design or build one's own furniture for children.

Although the standards do not legally apply to an individual making a piece of furniture, it would be foolish to ignore the safety standards or recommendations because the dangers exist regardless of who makes the piece. The majority of the safety material out there applies to the items that are involved in the most accidents. For the projects included here, that means cradles, cribs, bunk beds, and toy chests.

There are many basic rules for cradles and cribs, because these are almost the only places where a baby remains unattended for long periods of time. Most of the rules have

to do with preventing possible strangulation hazards. Dowels in the cradle sides and slats in the crib sides should be spaced no more than 2⅜ in. apart, so that the baby can't get either head or body (which will actually fit through smaller openings) through the space. These components should also be attached securely to the rails. Legs or posts should not project up more than ¹⁄₁₆ in. above any upper rail, headboard, or foot-board to prevent clothing from getting snagged during a fall. For the same reason, there shouldn't be any cut-out designs or notches that a child could get caught on or in.

The mattress should fit well into the cra-dle, crib, or bed, with no more than 1 in. of space around it, so the child cannot get wedged in between the mattress and the side of the bed and suffocate. The mattress support should be well secured so it cannot fall out of the frame. As with any project that is assembled with threaded fasteners, you should periodically check the tightness of all bolts and screws to be sure that they are secure. Another group of rules addresses the bedding and other accessories, but they are less of an issue to the furniture maker.

Bunk beds have rules for the size of any openings on the upper bunk, and guardrails are required on both sides of the top bunk. The guardrails must be attached securely to the bed. Any opening for access via the ladder should be no more than 15 in. In addition, the mattress support should be secured to the upper bunk side rails so that there is no chance for it and the mattress to dislodge and fall down, even when a child kicks up on the upper bunk from below. The safety standards also strongly suggest that children under six years old not sleep in the upper

Crib Safety: Headboard Cutouts

A cutout like this can trap a child's head.

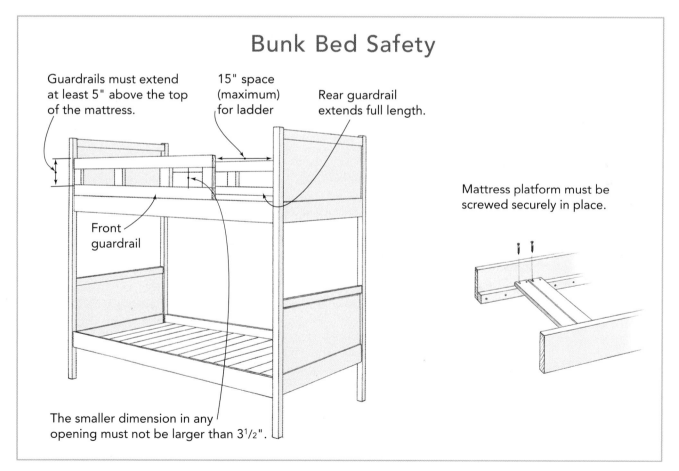

Bunk Bed Safety

Guardrails must extend at least 5" above the top of the mattress.

15" space (maximum) for ladder

Rear guardrail extends full length.

Front guardrail

Mattress platform must be screwed securely in place.

The smaller dimension in any opening must not be larger than 3½".

Toy-Chest Safety: Lid

Use a spring-and-cam lid support (not just a friction support) for the lid of a toy chest. The support should hold the lid in any position.

Toy-Chest Safety: Ventilation

A toy chest needs some form of ventilation—either a slot or holes—to allow a child to breath if he or she climbs inside and closes the lid.

Ventilation slot

Ventilation holes

bunk and that a night light be installed in a room with bunk beds, so the child can easily get out of bed in the middle of the night. Discouraging play on the upper bunk is also strongly suggested, but good luck enforcing that rule!

A toy chest should have a spring-loaded lid support to keep the lid from dropping down and smashing little fingers (or necks). There should also be some means to allow air to circulate inside the toy chest in case a child closes himself or herself inside the chest, a surprisingly common occurrence.

The Marble Chair (p. 106) is not subject to any specific standards, but it is not suitable for a child under three years old. Marbles are a dangerous choking hazard for children that young, who are still prone to ingest anything small enough to fit into their mouths. And, for that matter, be careful with marbles for any child, regardless of age, who tends to put objects in his or her mouth.

Commonsense Safety

In addition to the more critical safety issues discussed above, children bang into things. They bang into things hard. And this furniture is no different from any other that you might purchase in that regard. Good design won't keep children from crashing into or falling off of things, but it can help avoid needless trips to the emergency room. Corners should be rounded, to minimize the chance of a gash if someone bangs a head. Edges should be eased or rounded for the same reason. If the child who will be using the furniture is going through a particularly clumsy phase, it pays to look into some soft safety padding or bumpers.

I've tried to incorporate basic safety standards for the furniture in this book, and I've also tried to avoid other obvious problems. I've paid attention to our two children as they've used and abused their special furniture, and I've learned from being a parent and trying all kinds of commercially made children's stuff what works and what does not. Unfortunately, this doesn't eliminate all risk of accidents. And you need to use your common sense as well. If the child you're making something for is especially prone to banging into things, you should adjust the design accordingly. If you have other special concerns or the child has special needs, you have the option of modifying the designs to accommodate your own situation.

Safe Finishes

It may come as a surprise that most finishes for wood are considered safe enough for contact with food. Satisfying the requirements of the Food and Drug Administration in regard to food contact safety is not all that hard. Neither is it hard to meet the CPSC standard for crib finishes, which states that no crib may be finished with paint that contains more than 0.06 percent lead. However, convincing parents that something is safe for their newborn baby is another matter. This is not entirely without reason. Safe for contact with food is really not the same thing as edible, and infants and toddlers do tend to gnaw on and ingest things. I think that any discussion of the safety of finishes as they relate to children's furniture has to deal with both approaches. It is then for you to decide what to do based on your level of comfort and the age of the child.

Basically, most of the usual choices for finishing—shellac, lacquer, varnish, oil, and even paint—are considered safe once they have cured and all of the volatile solvents in them have evaporated or after the chemicals in them have combined to form inert substances. If you would like to use a particular finish, you should contact the manufacturer and ask specifically about whether it is suitable for the use you have in mind. Note that the labels on the container or even the Material Data Safety Sheet may not answer your question (unless there is a specific mention of unsuitability for use on children's furniture). Most of this information is about the nasty ingredients that will not necessarily be there after the finish has cured, but it is sometimes hard to distinguish between volatile solvents and various other ingredients. While you're talking to the manufacturer, ask how long it takes for the finish to cure completely. This curing process can take up to one month. Even finishes that are designed to be safe may need time to cure.

Since most parents are—at least at first—more than a little concerned about what their kids put in their mouths, you might want to go with one of a number of finishes that are unquestionably safe. Some of these are from companies that advertise the safety of their products. There is a whole industry built up around such products, and you'll find a wide range of finishes to choose from. You can purchase finishes specifically advertised as toy safe and others that are made with nontoxic ingredients and safe solvents. A good variety of safe finishes is available, from oils and waxes to paints, dyes, and stains. Other unquestionably safe finishes are old standards that happen to be natural and safe enough to eat. You can take either approach.

My current favorite is shellac. Shellac may not offer the same protection to the wood as a lacquer or a polyurethane, but it is a great-looking finish that will hold up reasonably

A small collection of available child-safe finishes. Many of the manufacturers of these products carry other finishes that are appropriate as well.

well. It can be fast and easy to apply. And it is actually edible. In fact, shellac is still used to coat some candies and medicines. For this level of safety, however, you have to mix up your own shellac from dried flakes and grain alcohol (ethanol). Most people, however, use denatured alcohol, which is ethanol made undrinkable (and less expensive because it is not subject to liquor taxes) by the addition of methanol or other toxic additives. Depending on the additives, you may not be comfortable with a toddler gnawing on the resultant finish. The variability of the formulations of denatured alcohol can compromise the quality of the finish. For the safest, highest-quality shellac finish, I mix it fresh, using the highest-proof grain alcohol I can find at my local liquor store. Coat the shellac with beeswax, an edible wax, and there are no worries.

Raw linseed oil and pure tung oil also work as completely safe finishes; boiled linseed oil contains metallic dryers and should not be used. Raw linseed oil dries very slowly (if at all), and I don't like it nearly as much as other possibilities. Pure tung oil is somewhat difficult to apply. Note that most products sold as a tung oil finish are oil/varnish blends, not pure tung oil.

Grain alcohol is an unlikely sight in the workshop, but it makes an excellent solvent for shellac. Denatured alcohol works, too.

Sizing Furniture for Children

Children come in a wide range of sizes and shapes, and their furniture should do so

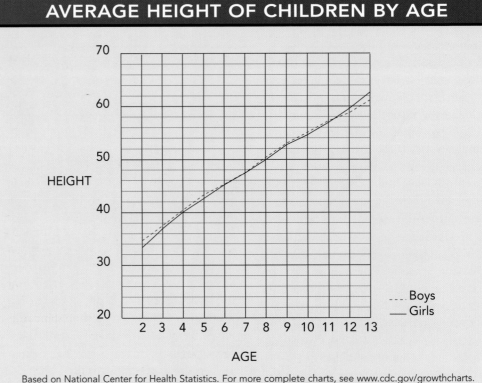

AVERAGE HEIGHT OF CHILDREN BY AGE

HEIGHT
AGE

---- Boys
—— Girls

Based on National Center for Health Statistics. For more complete charts, see www.cdc.gov/growthcharts.

too. This was the biggest challenge making my first piece of children's furniture. Knowing more about correct sizing for different ages ultimately helped me a lot. I discovered lots of charts and graphs and reference books. My favorite resource of this kind is *Humanscale 123,* by Niels Diffrient, Alvin R. Tilley, and Joan C. Bardagjy (MIT Press, 1974). This book has enough charts, dimensions, and specialized information to answer almost any question. And I also discovered that primary-school teachers tend to know what size chairs to order for their pupils and that I could easily measure up existing furniture that worked.

Ultimately, sizing furniture for children is a lot like buying clothing for children: You have to pick a particular size, and the child will either grow into it or grow out of it fairly rapidly. Luckily, furniture doesn't have to fit as well as clothing does. Take a look at the charts "Average Heights of Children by Age," "Children's Chair Heights," and "Children's Writing and School Table Sizes," but don't obsess about it.

Construction Basics

Children's furniture needs to be well made. Children may be smaller and lighter than adults, but adults don't use furniture as aggressively or as "creatively." Many of the projects shown here will be around for a long time as the child grows up and passed on to others, or used later in grown-up contexts. For these reasons, there isn't much room for compromises in the quality of construction. Make the pieces right, and not only will they hold up well but they'll be safer, too.

Good construction in many of the projects that follow means making mortise-and-tenon joints, because this joint is stronger and more durable than the common alternatives. The mortising block is a terrific jig for cutting mortises quickly, accurately, and repeatably. It works with a plunge router outfitted with a router fence. You'll use the mortising block for the Cradle, Crib, Panel Bed, Versatile Children's Table, and Marble Chair.

CHILDREN'S CHAIR HEIGHTS

Age (years)	Seat Height (in.)
2–4	9–11
4–7	10–15
7–10	13–17
10–13	15–18

Most children are comfortable in a wide range of chair sizes, use this chart as a guideline. The chair height is more important for writing at a desk than for playing. For writing and other work, the child should be able to sit comfortably with the feet flat on the floor and thighs supported on the chair seat (with generally good posture).

Note that the standard adult chair height is 18 in.

CHILDREN'S WRITING AND SCHOOL TABLE SIZES

Age (years)	Height (in.)
2–4	17–20
5–6	18–21
7–8	19–23
9–10	21–25
11–12	23–27
13+	24–30

The range in heights for each age reflects the disparities among different sources of information. Some ergonomics texts recommend the lower heights for tables. Play tables tend to be shorter, ranging from 16 in. to 18 in. in height. But most of the classrooms I investigated had tables that were at the taller end of the ranges.

Note that the standard adult table height is 28 in. to 30 in.

I show two possibilities for cutting tenons. Cutting tenons with the workpiece flat on the table saw is quick and requires a minimum of setup. But there will normally be some smoothing and a bit of fitting to get a good joint. The upright tenoning jig can be more accurate, but it requires attention to setup for the best results. The upright tenoning jig is used in building the Panel Bed and Marble Chair. This jig is a shop standard, and you can use it for completely different tasks as well.

The alignment-pin jig is used when building the Crib, the Child's Four-Poster

Mortising Block

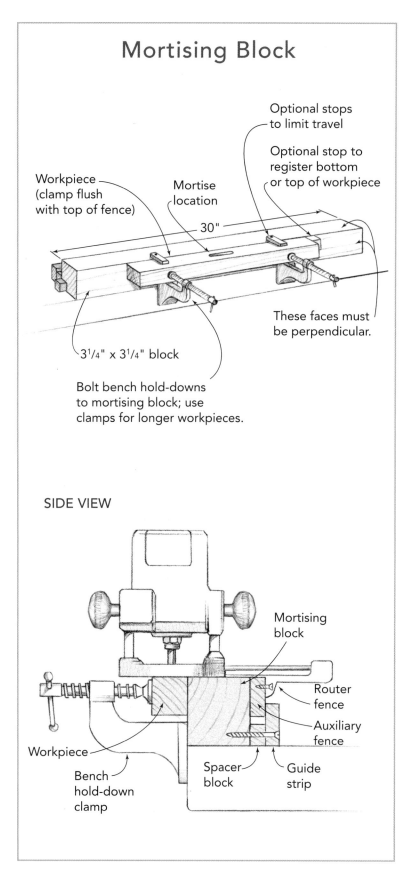

Optional stops to limit travel

Optional stop to register bottom or top of workpiece

Workpiece (clamp flush with top of fence)

Mortise location

30"

These faces must be perpendicular.

3¹/₄" x 3¹/₄" block

Bolt bench hold-downs to mortising block; use clamps for longer workpieces.

SIDE VIEW

Mortising block

Router fence

Auxiliary fence

Workpiece

Bench hold-down clamp

Spacer block

Guide strip

Bed, and the Panel Bed to make the bolted joints between the rails and the legs. These joints call for accurately matched holes for the dowels that serve as the alignment pins.

The Mortising Block

A plunge router equipped with a fence can easily and safely cut mortises in pieces wide enough to support the base of the router. The mortising block holds thin workpieces, allowing them to be mortised in the same way. The jig is essentially a large piece of wood milled flat and square that supports the router base during the cut.

Setting the fence controls the location of the mortise in the width of the stock. With the addition of a few simple stops screwed into place as needed, the location and size of the mortise along the length of the stock can be accurately controlled as well. Or you can simply rout by eye to lines drawn on the workpiece. A guide strip on the back keeps the router fence tight to the block during the cut.

With the workpiece clamped to the mortising block, you can safely rout narrow pieces. The router fence keeps the cut straight and located properly in the width of the stock. Stops position the cut in the length of the stock.

Tenons Flat on the Table Saw

It is easy to cut the tenon shoulders and waste away the cheeks by making repeated passes with the workpiece flat on the table saw. A wooden auxiliary fence attached to the miter guide extends beyond the blade and allows you to attach a stop block. Set this stop block to determine the length of the tenon (by setting the location of the tenon shoulder). The height of the blade, by determining the depth of the shoulder, controls the position and size of the tenon in the thickness of the workpiece.

Upright Tenoning Jig Cutting tenons with the workpiece held vertically has several advantages. The cheeks of the tenon can be cut cleanly, and in general, you can control the size of the tenon more accurately. But, unless you use a dado set to cut the cheeks (which works very well), you'll still have to cut the shoulders of the tenons and remove the waste pieces as a separate operation. **Caution:** Never use the miter guide and the rip fence together to cut off the waste pieces.

You can cut clean tenon shoulders and waste away the wood to the outside of the cheeks with the workpiece flat on the table saw. An auxiliary fence, clamped (or screwed) to the miter guide and a stop block are all you need to set up for this. Using a dado head is faster than cutting to the cheek with a single blade.

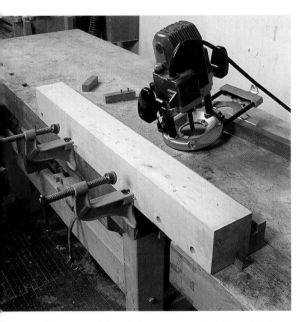

The mortising block is a valuable addition to your jig collection; with it you can rout slot mortises quickly and easily in a wide variety of pieces.

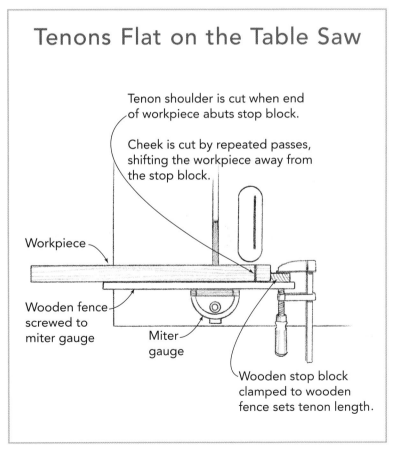

Tenons Flat on the Table Saw

Tenon shoulder is cut when end of workpiece abuts stop block.

Cheek is cut by repeated passes, shifting the workpiece away from the stop block.

Workpiece

Wooden fence screwed to miter gauge

Miter gauge

Wooden stop block clamped to wooden fence sets tenon length.

Upright Tenoning Jig

Screw jig together, being careful to keep screws away from where saw will cut.

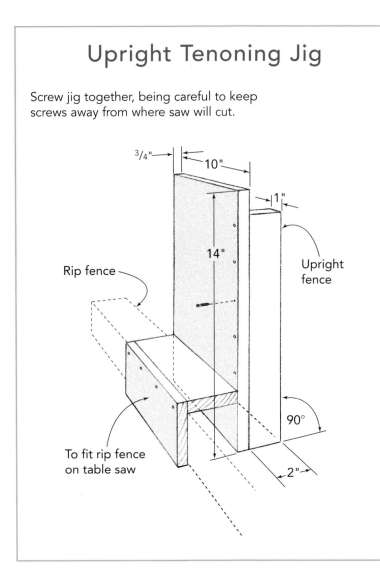

3/4"

10"

1"

14"

Rip fence

Upright fence

90°

2"

To fit rip fence on table saw

This will leave the waste piece dangerously trapped between the blade and the fence, and it will kick back with great force.

There are many commercially made tenoning jigs that work in basically the same way. The one shown at left slides along on the rip fence, and you control the location of the cuts by setting the rip fence.

The Alignment-Pin Jig

An alignment-pin jig is a straightforward device for drilling holes in the same locations on different pieces. The jig references off the 3⁄8-in. dowel in the middle. The 5⁄16-in.

The upright tenoning jig is easy to make and very versatile... if you don't already have a commercially made version.

Clamp the workpiece securely to the tenoning jig and make sure your clamp is well away from where the blade will cut. Here, I'm cutting with a dado set that I sharpened specially to cut flat-bottomed dadoes.

Alignment-Pin Jig

To use jig, insert locator dowel in bolt hole and line up jig parallel to post or rail. Clamp in place and drill the $^5/_{16}$" holes.

You can also use $^5/_{16}$"-inner-diameter metal bushings at the locations of each of the $^5/_{16}$" holes. The jig can then be made much thinner than $1^1/_4$".

holes to either side of it guide the drill bit when drilling the holes for the alignment pins ($^5/_{16}$-in. dowels) in the workpieces.

The jig can be made simply by drilling the holes in a block of hard maple on a drill press. Or you can improve the jig substantially by drilling oversize holes and inserting hardened steel sleeves ($^5/_{16}$-in. inner diameter) for the guide holes.

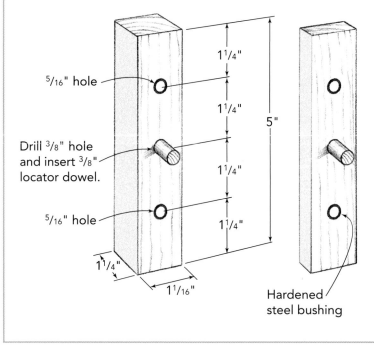

$^5/_{16}$" hole

Drill $^3/_8$" hole and insert $^3/_8$" locator dowel.

$^5/_{16}$" hole

$1^1/_4$"

$1^1/_4$"

$1^1/_4$"

$1^1/_4$"

5"

$1^1/_4$"

$1^1/_{16}$"

Hardened steel bushing

The alignment-pin jig (here fitted with $^5/_{16}$-in.-inner-diameter bushings) makes it easy to space and align the holes for bed rails and other parts that are bolted together.

KIDS IN THE SHOP

It's a lot of fun to show children what's going on in your shop, especially if you're making something just for them. But bringing a child into the shop is very risky. Direct and active supervision is required at all times. And allowing a child to watch you work does not constitute supervision. There is too much time when your attention must be focused on matters of your own safety. Can you guarantee that the child won't be curious about—and grab—this or that razor-sharp tool? Or find something interesting in some corner that could prove harmful?

But, having said all that, I do welcome my children (currently ages six and eight) into the shop when I'm not doing any work. We explore together, and I do some simple things with them. I want them to appreciate what I do and to learn the enjoyment of creating with wood. I just don't want them to get hurt because of something I did or didn't do in the dangerous workshop environment.

CRADLE

YEARS AGO, I FOUND IT hard to understand why anyone would want a cradle. Infants outgrow them in a matter of months, and then you need to get a crib and find a place for the cradle. Then we had our second child, who went through some rather fussy periods. I made a cradle. At night, I could try to calm her down without fully waking up myself just by reaching out and giving the cradle a gentle push, setting in motion the gentle, rhythmic rocking. There was also something comforting (perhaps more to us than to our daughter) about having her in a smaller, cozier bed. None of this completely solved her fussiness, but we loved having the cradle anyhow.

The cradle design is full of sinuous curves. On the more functional side, it features a nice stable base and has a reasonably good rock. It can also be partially disassembled, which makes it easier to store once it's time to put it away or to transfer it to someone else.

CRADLE

BECAUSE CRADLES DO get put away or passed along to the next baby in the family, this cradle is made to come apart, at least partially. The base disassembles and stores flat. The basket is just screwed together (though I've plugged the screw holes). If you want to make your cradle even easier to store, you can switch to the same kind of knockdown hardware used to connect the base uprights to the base stretcher. Don't use

screws and mushroom plugs—those plugs tend to fall out and could be a choking hazard.

The interior dimensions of the cradle basket—33¼" x 15¼"—accommodate the mattress I used. Be sure to verify the mattress size you will be using before beginning this project. The basket should be about ¼" larger (but no bigger) than the mattress.

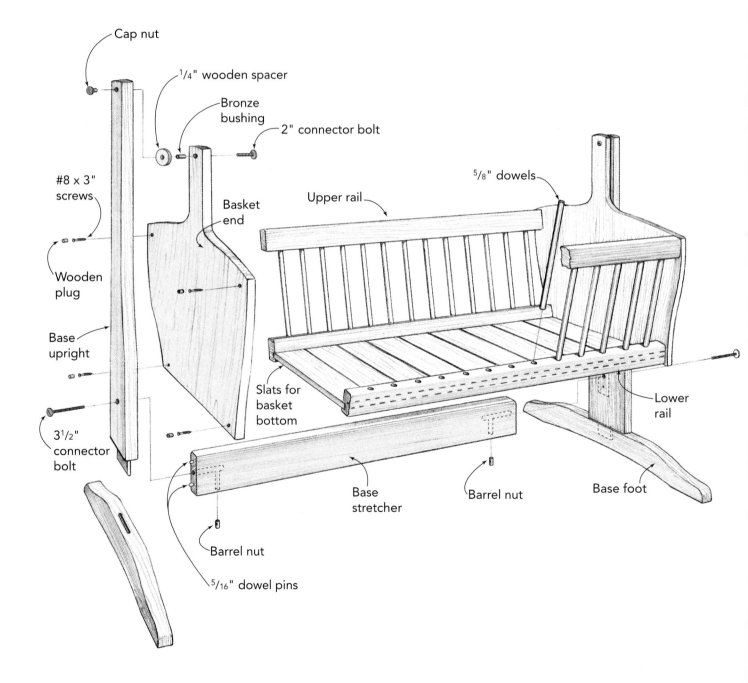

Cap nut

¼" wooden spacer

Bronze bushing

2" connector bolt

#8 x 3" screws

Basket end

Upper rail

⅝" dowels

Wooden plug

Base upright

Slats for basket bottom

Lower rail

3½" connector bolt

Base stretcher

Barrel nut

Base foot

Barrel nut

5/16" dowel pins

SIDE ELEVATION

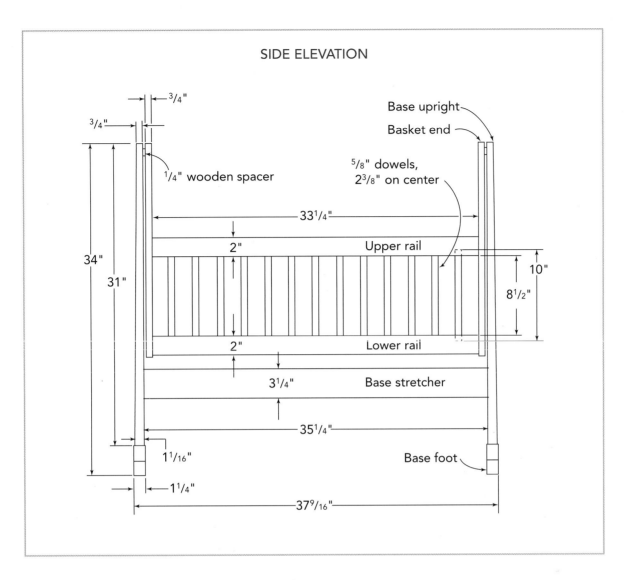

THE CRADLE BREAKS DOWN into two separate components—the swinging basket and the supporting frame. Each is built separately; then the basket is hung on the frame. It is best to begin by making full-scale patterns for all of the curved parts: the basket ends and the upright and horizontal base of the support frame.

Making the Patterns

Making up patterns out of ¼-in. plywood or similar material gives you a chance to draw out all of the parts full size and then easily refine the curves before you cut into any of your good wood. Sight carefully down each curve from both ends to confirm that the

curves flow well. Once you refine the curves on the pattern, the actual cutting and shaping go much easier.

1. Draw a grid of 1-in. squares onto a piece of ¼-in. plywood large enough for each pattern.

2. Enlarge the pattern for each of the parts by carefully transferring the pattern lines from "Cradle Patterns" on p. 21 to the grid on the plywood. To ensure symmetry it's best to make up just half patterns. You can then use the half patterns to trace both sides of each of the parts (see **Photo A** on p. 20).

3. Transfer the locations for the necessary holes onto the patterns.

4. Drill ³⁄₃₂-in. holes through the patterns so you can transfer the locations for the countersunk screw holes that will be used

CUT LIST FOR CRADLE

The Basket

2	Basket ends	¾" x 22" x 23"
4	Basket rails	1⅛" x 2" x 33¼"
26	Dowels	⅝" dia. x 10"
9	Slats	½" x 3⅝" x 16"
8	Dowels	⅜" x about 1"

The Base

2	Base uprights	1¹⁄₁₆" x 5" x 33½"
2	Base feet	1¼" x 3" x 26¼"
1	Base stretcher	1⅛" x 3¼" x 35¼"

Hardware

	Screws	#8 x 3"
2	Connector bolts (for base/stretcher assembly)	¼-20 x 3½"
2	Barrel nuts	¼-20
2	Connector bolts (for pivot joint)	¼-20 x 2"
2	Cap nuts for the connector bolts	
2	Bronze bushings	⁵⁄₁₆" o.d. x ¾"
2	Wooden spacers	1⅛" dia. x ¼" thick

Miscellaneous

8	Dowels (for alignment pins)	⁵⁄₁₆" dia.
	Scrap ¼-in. plywood for patterns	

PHOTO A: A half pattern is less work to make, and it is more likely to give you a symmetrical part. You do have to draw a centerline and reference the pattern off of that.

to attach the basket ends to the rails. The holes on the centerline are easy to transfer directly, but you can also cut or file notches in the centerline at the hole locations to simplify the layout.

Building the Basket

Start with the millwork for the basket ends and you can proceed with the remaining millwork while the glued-up blanks for the basket ends are still in clamps.

Making the basket ends

1. Mill the wood for the end panels ¾ in. thick. Then cut two pieces 3 in. by 23 in. and eight pieces 4¾ in. by 16 in. (see "Layout for Basket End Glue-Up" on p. 22). It is best if you can get all of the pieces for each end out of the same board. Failing that, look for a decent grain match.

2. Glue up the panels with the long board in the middle, keeping all of the boards flush on the end that will be the bottom of the basket.

3. When the glue has dried, level and smooth both faces of each panel.

4. Trace half of the basket end pattern onto the glued-up panel. Be sure to trace down the centerline of the pattern; then flip the pattern over and align it with the centerline to complete drawing the other half.

5. Mark the locations for all of the holes, as indicated, both in pencil and with a sharp awl.

6. Bandsaw the panels to shape, being careful to remain outside the layout lines.

7. Smooth the bandsawn edges with whatever combination of tools work for you (plane, spokeshave, rasp, etc.). The hardest part is in the curve from the basket proper to the stem. I used a 3-in. sanding drum mounted on my drill press (see **Photo B** on p. 22). I attached a piece of plywood with a 3¼-in. hole in it to my drill press table so I could drop the drum below the surface of the plywood and sand the entire edge.

8. Chamfer all edges (about ⅟₁₆ in.) with a router and chamfering bit. The chamfer should be about ⅟₁₆ in.

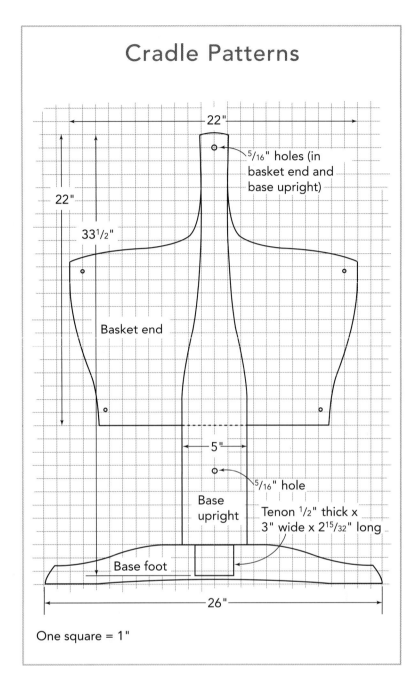

Cradle Patterns

22"

22"

33½"

$^{5}/_{16}$" holes (in basket end and base upright)

Basket end

5"

Base upright

$^{5}/_{16}$" hole

Tenon ½" thick x 3" wide x 2$^{15}/_{32}$" long

Base foot

26"

One square = 1"

TIP

Wait overnight for the glue to dry before planing, scraping, or sanding the faces. Moisture from the glue in the joint will swell that area temporarily. If you don't wait for the wood to subside before you level and smooth the surface, you'll have slightly sunken areas around each glueline when it does dry.

Layout for Basket End Glue-Up

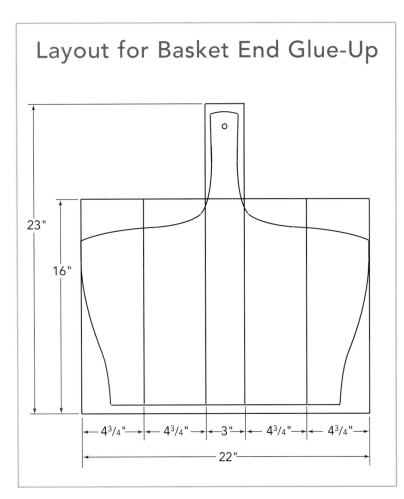

23"

16"

4³/₄" — 4³/₄" — 3" — 4³/₄" — 4³/₄"

22"

PHOTO B: The part of the basket end that's hard to sand by hand is easy to sand with a sanding drum mounted in the drill press.

9. Drill the ⁵/₁₆-in. pivot hole at the marked location at the top of the stem. Be sure that the hole is centered on the basket end.

10. Drill countersunk pilot holes for the screws in the specified locations for attaching the upper and lower basket rails. Drill the holes from the outside of the basket ends and countersink just deeply enough to allow for plugging after assembly.

Making the Basket Sides

Each basket side consists of an upper and lower rail and 13 spindles, made from ⅝-in. cherry dowel stock.

Cutting the rails

1. Mill the stock for the four rails to size; then cut them to length.

2. Lay out the dowel-hole locations on each of the rails. This is a good time to mark out which rail goes where as well as the inside and outside faces of each. It can get confusing once you start drilling.

3. Before setting up to drill the rails, test your drill bit by drilling into a scrap of the same wood to check the fit of your dowels. If it is consistently off, you can use a slightly different size drill bit. Note that a 16mm bit is 0.005 in. bigger and can save you some time fitting the dowels.

4. On the table saw, cut a drill-press jig for orienting the rails to drill the angled holes (see "Jig for Drilling Angled Holes in the Rails").

5. Mount the jig on your drill-press so that the holes will be centered on the top edge of the rails. Set the drill-press stop to produce a ¼-in.-deep hole. Drill the rails as shown (see **Photo C**).

6. In the bottom of the outermost holes on each rail, drill a ⅜-in. hole straight down (without the angled jig). Don't drill through the rail; stop about ¼ in. short of the opposite side. Insert a ⅜-in. dowel into each of these holes. Make sure the dowels don't stick up into the ⅝-in. part of the holes (see "Detail of Outer Holes in Rails").

Detail of Outer Holes in Rails

CROSS SECTION

Hole for ⁵/₈" dowel

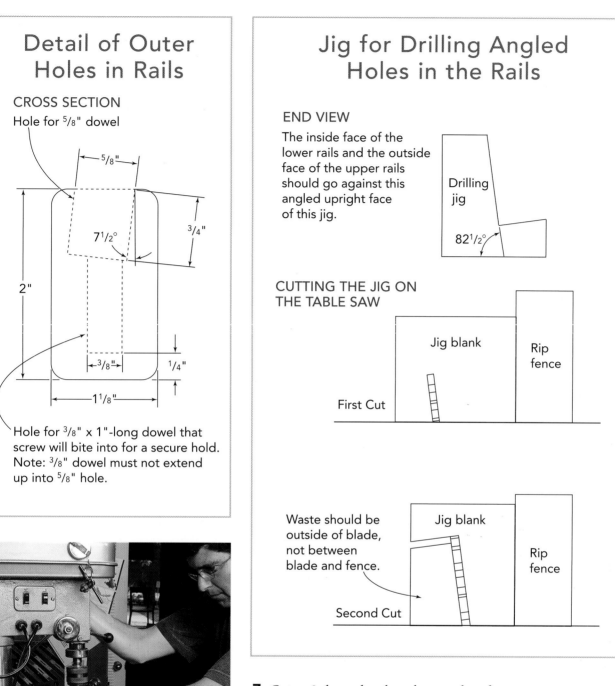

5/8"

3/4"

7¹/₂°

2"

³/₈"

1/4"

1¹/₈"

Hole for ³/₈" x 1"-long dowel that screw will bite into for a secure hold. Note: ³/₈" dowel must not extend up into ⁵/₈" hole.

PHOTO C: Clamp the angled drilling fence to the drill-press table to drill the ⅝-in. holes centered on the rails.

Jig for Drilling Angled Holes in the Rails

END VIEW

The inside face of the lower rails and the outside face of the upper rails should go against this angled upright face of this jig.

Drilling jig

82¹/₂°

CUTTING THE JIG ON THE TABLE SAW

Jig blank

Rip fence

First Cut

Waste should be outside of blade, not between blade and fence.

Jig blank

Rip fence

Second Cut

7. Cut an 8-degree bevel on the top edge of the two upper rails (cutting the wood off the outside corner) so the rail matches the shape of the basket ends. Be sure to check that you indeed have the two upper rails and that the longer side of each rail will be on the inside (see "Cradle Rail Details" on p. 24).

8. Cut the grooves for the cradle bottom on the inside faces of the two lower rails. The grooves are ½ in. wide, ⅜ in. deep, and

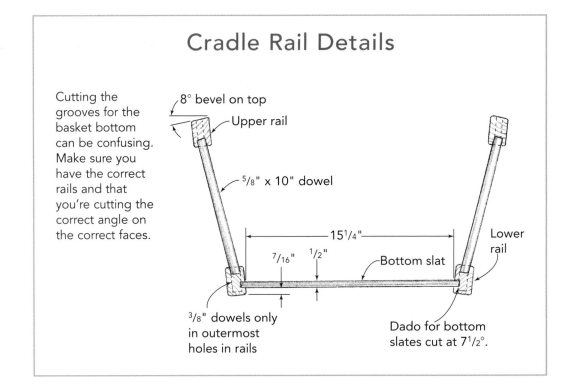

Cradle Rail Details

Cutting the grooves for the basket bottom can be confusing. Make sure you have the correct rails and that you're cutting the correct angle on the correct faces.

8° bevel on top

Upper rail

5/8" x 10" dowel

15 1/4"

7/16"   1/2"

Bottom slat

Lower rail

3/8" dowels only in outermost holes in rails

Dado for bottom slates cut at 7 1/2°.

PHOTO D: The actual length of the dowels should be determined by checking the result of a test-assembly against the basket ends.

angled at 7½ degrees (see "Detail of Outer Holes in Rails" on p. 23). Take your time figuring out where this groove goes before you cut.

Cutting the dowels

Before you cut all of the ⅝-in. dowels to length, you need to be sure you have the right measurement.

1. Cut a pair of dowels to 10 in. long; then insert them into the first and last holes on the rails from one side. Hold this side assembly up to a basket end to see if the rails are positioned properly. There should be ⅛ in. to 5⁄32 in. above and below the rails (see **Photo D**). Adjust the dowel length if necessary.

2. Cut all 26 dowels to length.

3. Sand the ends of the dowels as necessary to fit into the holes.

Making the basket bottom

Although the bottom of the basket could easily be made out of ½-in. plywood, I chose to use maple slats because I prefer the look. This also eliminates any chance of formaldehyde out-gassing from the glues used to make some plywoods. You'll need to leave a bit of room for the slats to expand with any increase in humidity. The combined width of all of the slats should be ½ in. to ¾ in. less than the length of the side rails.

1. Mill up the material for the slats out of maple or a similarly strong wood. You'll need nine pieces roughly 3⅝ in. wide by ½ in. thick by 16 in. long, but mill up some extras. When you're milling them, be sure to check the fit of the slats in the rail grooves. They should slide in without trouble but should not be loose. Save some of the scrap to insert into the grooves when you clamp up the sides of the basket, to protect the groove from being crushed by the clamps.

2. Round over all four edges by routing with a ⅛-in. roundover bit or just sand the edges smooth.

3. Before cutting the slats to length, check the length in place: Cut two pieces of extra slat material and put them into the grooves on the basket sides, one at each end. Hold a basket end up to this assembly and make sure there is about ⅛ in. of end panel outside the rails. Adjust the slat length if necessary; then cut all the slats to length.

Assembling the basket

1. Go over all of the parts to be sure they are well sanded—it's harder to sand once everything is together. It's also easier to finish some of these parts before the final assembly. This isn't necessary, and I didn't do any prefinishing when I made the cradle shown here. In any event, leave the outsides of the basket ends for later, because you still have to plug the screw holes—and cutting these off flush will mar the finish on the surrounding surfaces. You can leave the bottom slats completely unfinished.

2. Get ready for the assembly process by setting up all of the necessary clamps with either clamp pads or cauls. Then carefully lay out the proper parts so you can put them together correctly. The differences between the rails are subtle, so check carefully. Also, get your glue, a piece of a small (¼-in.- to ½-in.-diameter) dowel to use as a glue spreader, and a scrap of the slat stock you

PHOTO E: Insert all of the dowels into one of the lower side rails first.

PHOTO F: The upper rail goes on to the lower rail and dowels one dowel at a time, starting at one end. Once the dowels are all in place, clamp the rails to be sure the dowels seat all the way.

will use to fill the groove in the lower rails and keep the wood from cracking as you clamp across this groove.

3. Apply a little bit of glue into each of the holes in one rail by using the dowel glue spreader. Use your glue sparingly to avoid squeeze-out.

4. Insert all of the dowels into their holes (see **Photo E**); then spread glue in the holes in the appropriate rail. Starting at one end, work the dowels into the holes in the other rail, one at a time (see **Photo F**).

PHOTO G: Keep one corner of the basket end off the edge of your workbench to give you access to the screw.

TIP

Work on the joinery for the base parts while the parts are still rectangular blanks; it's much easier than cutting the joints on the already shaped parts.

5. Insert the scrap of slat stock into the groove; then clamp up the side, placing clamps on both sides of the basket side assembly.

6. Assemble the other side of the basket in the same way. Leave the assemblies clamped until the glue has set.

7. Insert the slats for the basket bottom into one basket side; then work the slats into the groove in the other side. Use another set of hands—that is, some tape, a big rubber band, or a clamp applied lightly—to help hold things together.

8. Place one of the basket ends on the bench, inside facing up and with a corner hanging over the edge of the bench. Tip the basket sides-and-bottom assembly up onto the basket end. Align the basket sides so that they are centered on the basket end, judging by eye or using a ruler. (You could do this the other way around: Place the basket sides-and-bottom assembly on the floor, position

the basket end on top, and drill down into the rails. But that makes it more difficult to ensure that the assembly is centered on the basket end.)

9. Using a bit the same diameter as the root of the #8 by 3-in. screws you'll use for assembly, drill a pilot hole in the rail, up through the countersunk hole in the basket end. Drive in a screw (see **Photo G**).

10. Repeat this process with all of the other holes for the assembly screws on one basket end; then carefully turn the basket over and do the same thing with the other end.

11. Plug all of the screw holes. Once the glue has dried, trim the plugs off with either a saw or a chisel; then sand the plugs flush.

Building the Base

The base is much simpler to make than the basket; there are two mortise-and-tenon joints to cut for the base uprights, and the two uprights simply bolt to the stretcher.

Making the base uprights

1. Mill and cut the blanks for the base uprights to size.

2. Lay out the mortise centered on each of the feet as well as the location of the tenon on the bottom of each of the uprights.

3. Cut the mortises in the feet. I like using a plunge router outfitted with a fence in conjunction with a jig I call a mortising block (see "Mortising Block" on p. 12).

4. Cut a tenon on the bottom of each of the uprights—I did this on the table saw—and fit carefully to the mortises.

5. Trace out the shapes of the base feet and uprights using the patterns you made earlier and bandsaw to shape. Leave the tops of the uprights long for now. Mark the locations for the two holes in each of the uprights.

6. Smooth the curved edges with sandpaper and a curved sanding block. If you have one, a compass plane or a spokeshave can do the job even quicker.

7. The outside face of each of the uprights tapers, so the upright, which is 1¹⁄₁₆ in. thick where it joins the foot, is ¾ in. thick at the

26 ✦ CRADLE

top. I did the tapering by handplaning, but you could make up a sled to taper the uprights in a planer or you could even cut the taper on the bandsaw before shaping the uprights. After you taper the uprights, be sure to mark the tapered side on one of the edges or on the tenon at the bottom. It is almost impossible to tell which side is tapered later, and it's important that the tapered side faces out.

8. Drill both the pivot and the bolt holes using a ⁵⁄₁₆-in. bit in a drill press. Make sure the tapered side is up.

9. Mark the exact shape of the top of the upright directly from the cradle basket by sticking the bottom end of a drill bit or a ⁵⁄₁₆-in. dowel through the holes in both parts to align them and then marking with a sharp pencil (see **Photo H**). Cut the top of the upright and smooth exactly to the line. If you want to check the match, you can slip the drill bit back into the holes and check the alignment; you can even do a little sanding while the parts are held in alignment.

10. Enlarge the pivot hole to 9mm (or ²³⁄₆₄ in.). This is the size of the cap nut (the female part of the connector bolt set).

11. Glue and clamp the uprights to the feet.

Making the base stretcher

1. Mill the stretcher to size. Verify the length by adding ⁹⁄₁₆ in. to the length of the basket as measured outside to outside at the top of the basket end stems.

2. Drill the holes for the connector bolts first, using a self-centering dowel jig to be sure you bore a straight, centered ⅜-in. hole in each of the ends of the stretcher.

3. Drill the holes for the alignment pins next (see "Base Stretcher" on p. 28). The alignment pins are simply short pieces of ⁵⁄₁₆-in. dowel that keep the stretcher from twisting. I drilled the holes using the self-centering dowel jig again, locating the ⁵⁄₁₆-in.-diameter holes by sticking a ⅜-in. drill bit into the ⅜-in. hole on the jig and then into the bolt hole on the stretcher. On my jig, this put the ⁵⁄₁₆-in. hole just over ½ in. away from the bolt hole, but anything that isn't too close to the edge of the stretcher will work.

PHOTO H: Scribe the top of the base uprights directly from the basket ends so they match perfectly.

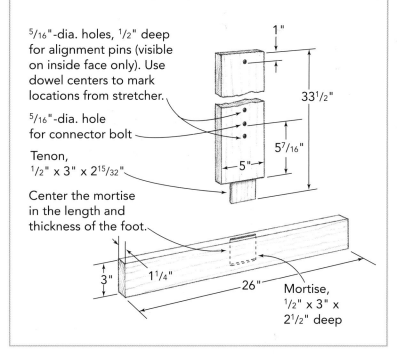

Base Upright and Foot

⁵⁄₁₆"-dia. holes, ½" deep for alignment pins (visible on inside face only). Use dowel centers to mark locations from stretcher.

⁵⁄₁₆"-dia. hole for connector bolt

Tenon, ½" x 3" x 2¹⁵⁄₃₂"

Center the mortise in the length and thickness of the foot.

1"

33½"

5⁷⁄₁₆"

5"

3"

1¼"

26"

Mortise, ½" x 3" x 2½" deep

Base Stretcher

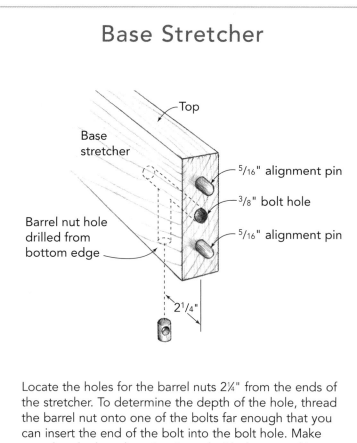

Top

Base stretcher

5/16" alignment pin

3/8" bolt hole

5/16" alignment pin

Barrel nut hole drilled from bottom edge

2¹/₄"

Locate the holes for the barrel nuts 2¼" from the ends of the stretcher. To determine the depth of the hole, thread the barrel nut onto one of the bolts far enough that you can insert the end of the bolt into the bolt hole. Make sure that the barrel nut is oriented with the screwdriver slot facing up; then measure the distance from the top of the crossrail to the bottom of the nut. This will be the depth of the drilled hole for the nut. You can set the depth of cut on the drill press directly from this.

Drilling for Barrel Nuts

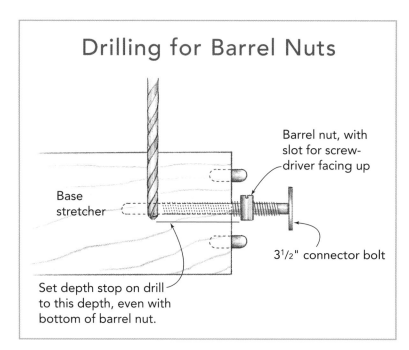

Barrel nut, with slot for screw-driver facing up

Base stretcher

3¹/₂" connector bolt

Set depth stop on drill to this depth, even with bottom of barrel nut.

Drill two 5/16-in. holes on each end, flipping the dowel jig around to locate the second hole. The holes should be about 1 in. deep.

4. Drill the 10mm holes for the barrel nuts, as shown in "Drilling for Barrel Nuts."

5. Use dowel centers to locate the alignment-pin holes in the base uprights. Place the dowel centers in the two 5/16-in. holes in the stretcher; then insert the connector bolt through the upright and into the rail. Align the stretcher carefully so that it is straight and press the pointed ends of the dowel centers into the upright. Drill 5/16-in. holes centered on each of these points using a drill press. Set the depth stop on the drill press carefully to be sure the holes go no deeper than ½ in.

6. Glue dowels into the 5/16-in. holes in the stretcher and trim if necessary so they stick out about ⅜ in. Chamfer the ends of the dowels with a pencil sharpener (a very useful tool for pointing or chamfering the ends of dowels) or some sandpaper.

7. Bolt the base together with the connector bolts and barrel nuts.

Hanging the Basket

Making the wooden spacers

1. Drill three or four holes partway through a 2-in.- or 3-in.-wide, ¾-in.-thick board with a 1⅜-in. hole saw or an adjustable fly cutter (you want a disk that is about 1⅛ in. in diameter). Redrill the center holes to enlarge them to 5/16 in.

2. Set the rip fence on the table saw so there is ¼ in. of this board to the outside of the blade. Raise the blade height so that it will cut through the disks. The disks will fall out to the waste side of the cut when you rip the board (see **Photo I**).

3. Sanding the spacers can be done by hand, but I cut the head off of a 5/16-in. bolt, threaded a nut and washer on and then one of the wooden spacers, and finally tightened on another washer and nut. Chucking this assembly into the drill press, I was able to sand the edges smooth very quickly.

PHOTO I: Cutting the drilled spacers out of the block is a straightforward process on the table saw.

Installing the pivot hardware

Photo J shows the pivot hardware pieces; see also "Basket Pivot Detail."

1. Insert the ⁵⁄₁₆-in.-outer-diameter by ¾-in.-long bronze bushings through the holes in the basket ends from the outside; leave about ¼ in. sticking out. Fit the wooden spacers over the protruding part of the bushings.

2. Insert the cap nuts (the female side of the connector bolt) into the uprights on the base.

3. Hold the basket up in position (you may want some extra help with this) and insert the male part of the connector bolt from inside the basket end. Tighten securely.

4. You will probably find that the bolt won't tighten down all the way because it's too long. Measure the size of the gap, disassemble the hardware, and place the basket aside. Cut the bolt down by the amount of the gap minus ¹⁄₃₂ in. or more. The goal is to have the connector bolt tightly assembled without binding the swing of the basket at all. If you cut the bolt too short and the basket binds, try putting a thin piece of metal into the cap nut to make the bolt/nut combination a little longer.

Finishing

Finish the cradle and let the finish cure for the appropriate amount of time before you plan to use it.

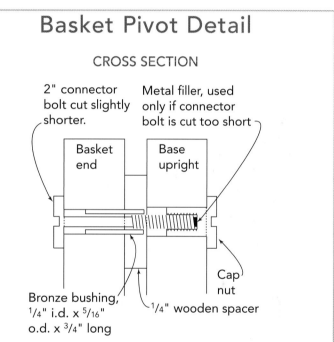

Basket Pivot Detail

CROSS SECTION

2" connector bolt cut slightly shorter.

Metal filler, used only if connector bolt is cut too short

Basket end

Base upright

Bronze bushing, ¼" i.d. x ⁵⁄₁₆" o.d. x ¾" long

Cap nut

¼" wooden spacer

PHOTO J: The pivot is put together from stuff I found at my local hardware store. One of the connector bolts is cut shorter so that it can be tightened down all the way.

CRIB

YOU MIGHT NOT NEED A CRADLE for a baby, but you'll certainly need a crib. And this crib is one that can be passed on to subsequent children, and then on and on throughout the family. My version of this crib has seen four children over the last eight years: my two and two nephews.

When I first made this crib there were no bolts. I just glued it all together. While my wife was still in the hospital, I proudly brought it home and wrestled it up the stairs, only to find that it would not fit through the door to the baby's room. Humbled, I struggled back down the stairs and back to the shop, where I had to bash the ends off and then drill for the bolts. Lesson learned. Bolting the crib together also means that you can unbolt it and store it or send it along to another family member.

Leave enough time to make this project if you're expecting your own child to use it. There are lots of mortise-and-tenon joints to cut. You could stall a little and keep a newborn in something more temporary, but this is bound to create some tension at home.

CRIB

THE CRIB IS MADE OF FIVE assemblies (the two ends, the back, the front gate, and the mattress platform) and a rail. Most of these components bolt together to create a rigid frame. The front drop gate is the exception; it slides up and down in a special groove in the front legs.

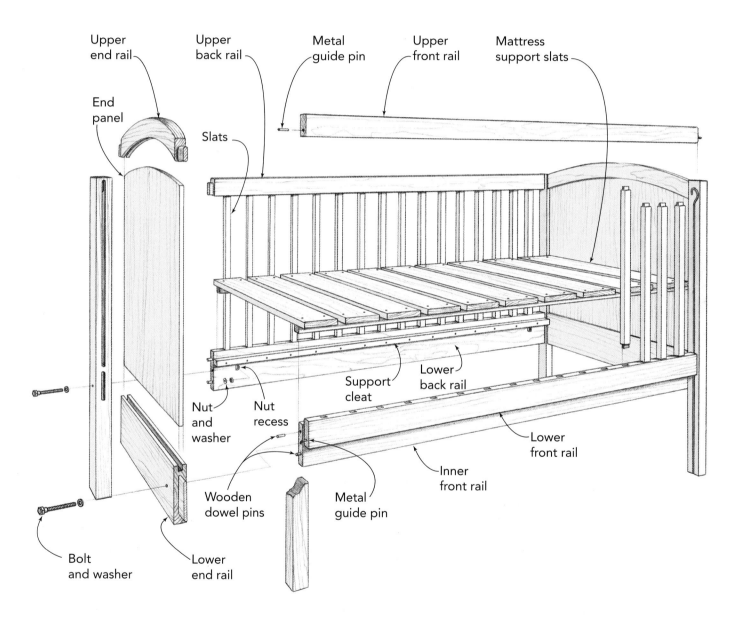

Upper end rail

End panel

Upper back rail

Metal guide pin

Upper front rail

Mattress support slats

Slats

Nut and washer

Nut recess

Support cleat

Lower back rail

Lower front rail

Inner front rail

Wooden dowel pins

Metal guide pin

Bolt and washer

Lower end rail

END SECTION

Upper front rail

Upper back rail

Upper end rail

Slat

Matress support slat

Lower front rail

Lower back rail

Support cleat

Inner front rail

Slat rails

Bottom of shepherd's-hook groove

END VIEW

2 1/2" rise

2"

3/8" bolt hole with 3/4" counterbore

5"

40"

2"

10"

12 1/2"

27 1/4"

30 3/4"

FRONT VIEW

Upper end rail

Upper front rail

1"

2 1/8"

1 1/8"

2 3/4"

12 1/4"

10"

Inner front rail

Lower front rail

1 3/4"

51 9/16"

55 1/16"

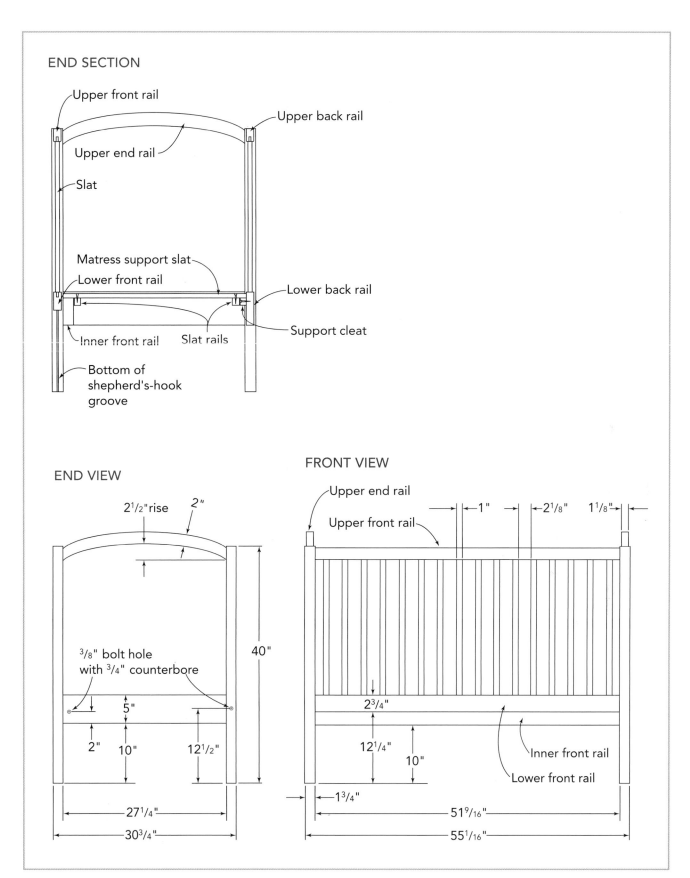

CUT LIST FOR CRIB	
4 Legs	1¾" x 1¾" x 40"
2 Lower end rails	1⅛" x 5" x 30¼"
2 Upper end rails	1⅛" x 4½" x 30¼"
2 End panels	½" x 28¼" x 26½"
1 Upper back rail	1⅛" x 2" x 52 9/16"
1 Lower back rail	1⅛" x 5" x 51 9/16"
1 Upper front rail	1⅛" x 2" x 51 17/32"
1 Lower front rail	1⅛" x 2¾" x 51 17/32"
1 Inner front rail	1⅛" x 4" x 52 3/16"
32 Slats	⅝" x 1" x 24¼"
1 Support cleat	1" x 1" x 51½"
2 Slat rails	1" x 1" x 51¼"
10 Mattress-support slats	¾" x 4" x 27 9/16"
Hardware	
4 Bolts with nuts	5/16" x 5½"
8 Washers	5/16" SAE*
8 Dowels (for alignment pins)	5/16" x 1¼"
4 Metal rods	¼" x 1¾"
Screws	#6 x 1¼"
2 Screw-on rubber bumpers	⅝" or ¾" dia.
Miscellaneous	
Scrap plywood for pattern	¼" thick

*These have a slightly larger hole than standard 5/16" washers. Most hardware stores and auto parts stores carry them.

TIP

Rout the groove in several shallow passes instead of one full-depth pass. This makes a smoother, more accurate cut.

THIS CRIB COMES APART into sections, which makes it easy to store or ship and a little easier to build. You can do each component as a separate project.

Making the Legs

All of the legs are the same size, 1¾ in. square by 40 in. long. Be sure the legs are straight and square before continuing on with the joinery. See "Mortise and Hole Locations for the Legs" for laying out the joinery.

Drilling for the bolts on the back legs

I like to drill the holes for the bolts from both sides of the leg, measuring carefully first so that I'm sure I'm drilling along the same axis. Drilling from both sides ensures that the holes will be where you want them. Otherwise, the drill can wander.

1. Measure up 12½ in. from the bottom of each of the two back legs on both the inside and the outside. Then carefully mark out the centerpoint of the legs on these marks.

2. Drill from the outside with a ¾-in. flat-bottomed bit (such as a Forstner bit) 7/16 in. deep. Then drill with a ⅜-in. drill bit about 1 in. deeper. Turn the leg over and drill with the ⅜-in. bit until you reach the hole from the other side. Run the bit through the hole to even out any discrepancy.

3. Now drill the two 5/16-in. by 1-in.-deep holes for the alignment pins. You can use the custom drilling jig shown in "Alignment-Pin Jig" on p. 15 or mark out and drill with a self-centering dowel jig.

Cutting the leg mortises

All four of the legs get mortises for the end rails (both the upper rails and the lower rails) in the same locations. So once you set up to cut one, you can cut all four. In addition, the back legs have shallower mortises to hold the upper back rail in place. You can cut these with the same setup that you use for the upper end-rail mortises. Be sure to locate these on the proper faces. See "Mortising Block" on p. 12 for a convenient mortising jig.

Routing the shepherd's-hook grooves

1. Place a pencil mark on the facing sides of the two front legs $^{11}/_{32}$ in. down from the top. This is where the top of the routing jig needs to go so the groove will end up $^{7}/_{16}$ in. below the top of the leg.

2. Clamp the template (see "A Template for Routing the Shepherd's-Hook Grooves" on p. 36) into place and rout, using a combination of a $^{1}/_{4}$-in. bit and a $^{7}/_{16}$-in. guide bushing on the router. Rout the groove $^{5}/_{16}$ in. deep (see **Photo A**).

3. Unscrew the fence from the shepherd's-hook routing jig, clamp it in position on the other side of the jig, and screw it into place there. Be sure the screws are below the surface of the jig.

PHOTO A: Mount a $^{7}/_{16}$-in. guide bushing and a $^{1}/_{4}$-in. straight bit in the router to rout the shepherd's-hook groove on the top of the leg.

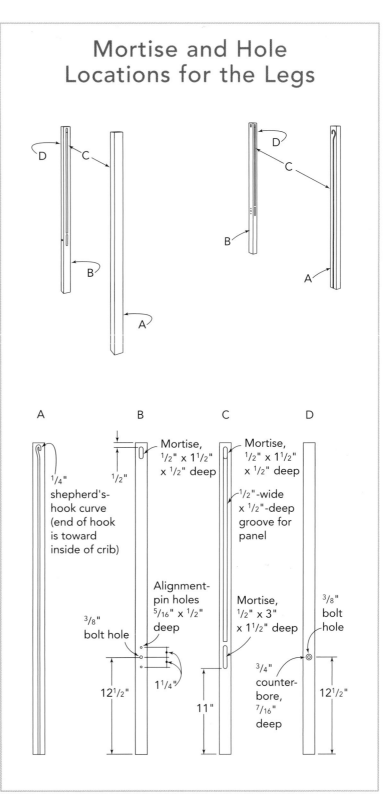

Mortise and Hole Locations for the Legs

A — $^{1}/_{4}$" shepherd's-hook curve (end of hook is toward inside of crib)

B — Mortise, $^{1}/_{2}$" x $1^{1}/_{2}$" x $^{1}/_{2}$" deep
$^{1}/_{2}$"
Alignment-pin holes $^{5}/_{16}$" x $^{1}/_{2}$" deep
$^{3}/_{8}$" bolt hole
$12^{1}/_{2}$"
$1^{1}/_{4}$"

C — Mortise, $^{1}/_{2}$" x $1^{1}/_{2}$" x $^{1}/_{2}$" deep
$^{1}/_{2}$"-wide x $^{1}/_{2}$"-deep groove for panel
Mortise, $^{1}/_{2}$" x 3" x $1^{1}/_{2}$" deep
$^{3}/_{4}$" counter-bore, $^{7}/_{16}$" deep
11"

D — $^{3}/_{8}$" bolt hole
$12^{1}/_{2}$"

A TEMPLATE FOR ROUTING THE SHEPHERD'S-HOOK GROOVES

Making the template is best as a two-step process. The first step is to make a preliminary pattern for routing the hook. Then you use that pattern to make the actual jig. Making the pattern in thinner stock first makes it easier to get a precise shape that fits a router guide bushing perfectly.

1. Trace the hook pattern onto a piece of ¼-in. plywood approximately 10 in. by 15 in.

2. Bandsaw out the inside of the pattern, getting as close to the lines as possible without touching them. Nibble away at the wood inside the lines so that you can cut the entire pattern and exit through the same kerf.

3. Screw or nail a wooden strip across the entrance/exit kerf.

4. File or sand the inside of the pattern smooth, checking that a ⁷⁄₁₆-in. guide bushing just fits along the entire length of the pattern.

5. Now it's time to make the actual template. Clamp or screw the pattern onto a piece of ½-in.-thick plywood or medium-density fiberboard (MDF), drill a ⅜-in. hole through this template stock in the middle of the pattern for a flush-trimming router bit to start, and rout the hook onto the template.

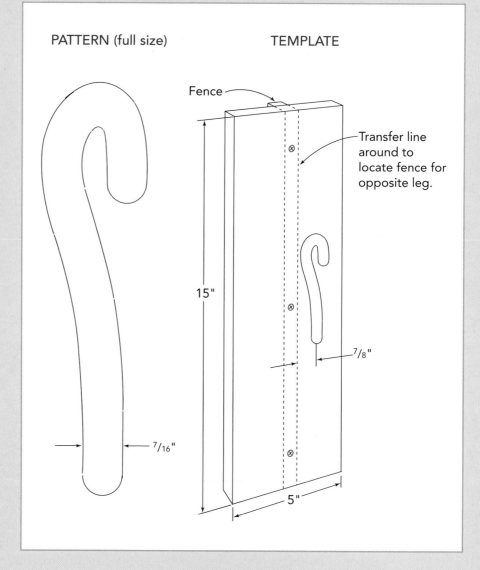

PATTERN (full size)

TEMPLATE

Fence

Transfer line around to locate fence for opposite leg.

15"

⁷⁄₈"

⁷⁄₁₆"

5"

To make the hook jig (right), begin by making a pattern (left).

PHOTO B: Cutting the straight part of the groove down the leg calls for using the router fence. Line up the groove carefully with the bottom of the hook.

6. Add a fence to locate the bottom straight part of the template the right distance from the edge of the crib leg. The center of the pattern should be exactly ⅞ in. from the fence. Screw the fence in place; then transfer the location around to the opposite side of the template. When you rout the opposite leg, you'll unscrew the fence from one side and place it on the other side of the template so each shepherd's-hook groove is oriented with the hook toward the inside of the crib.

4. Place the jig in position on the opposite leg and rout the groove.

5. Rout the rest of the ¼-in. groove straight down the leg all the way to the bottom. I set another leg next to the leg I was routing to provide some stability for the router and then used a router with a fence (see **Photo B**). Set up carefully so the groove meets the bottom of the hook perfectly. Rout the groove in a few shallow passes, rather than all at once. Be sure the final depth matches that in the hook portion of the groove.

Making the Rails

Mill the stock for all of the rails to 1⅛ in. thick. Rip the pieces to width according to the cut list, but leave all of the rail stock long for now. Mark each piece clearly so you know what it is and where it goes on the crib.

Rail Details

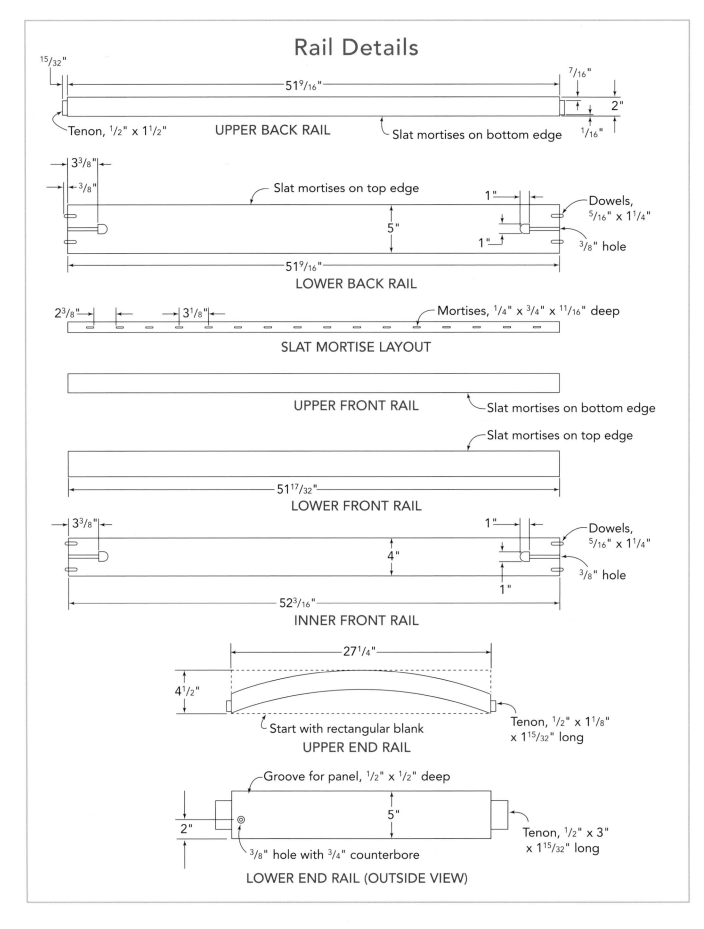

15/32"

51⁹/₁₆"

7/16"

2"

1/16"

Tenon, 1/2" x 1¹/₂"   UPPER BACK RAIL   Slat mortises on bottom edge

3³/₈"

3/8"

Slat mortises on top edge

1"

Dowels,
5/16" x 1¹/₄"

5"

1"

3/8" hole

51⁹/₁₆"

LOWER BACK RAIL

2³/₈"   3¹/₈"   Mortises, 1/4" x ³/₄" x ¹¹/₁₆" deep

SLAT MORTISE LAYOUT

UPPER FRONT RAIL   Slat mortises on bottom edge

Slat mortises on top edge

51¹⁷/₃₂"

LOWER FRONT RAIL

3³/₈"   1"   Dowels,
5/16" x 1¹/₄"

4"

3/8" hole

1"

52³/₁₆"

INNER FRONT RAIL

27¹/₄"

4¹/₂"

Tenon, 1/2" x 1¹/₈"
x 1¹⁵/₃₂" long

Start with rectangular blank
UPPER END RAIL

Groove for panel, 1/2" x 1/2" deep

5"

2"

Tenon, 1/2" x 3"
x 1¹⁵/₃₂" long

3/8" hole with ³/₄" counterbore

LOWER END RAIL (OUTSIDE VIEW)

Making the lower end rails

1. Determine the overall length of the two lower end rails by adding the tenon lengths (½2 in. less than the actual mortise depths in the legs) to the desired distance between the legs, which is 27¼ in.

2. Mark out the tenons, centered both side to side and top to bottom (see "Rail Details").

3. Cut the tenons using your preferred method. I used a tenoning jig on the table saw to cut them.

4. I find it easier to round over the ends of the tenons to fit the routed mortises than to square up the mortises. A rasp can accomplish the job quickly.

5. Fit each tenon carefully to its mortise; then mark both with a letter or number so you know what goes where.

Making the upper end rails

The upper end rails should be the same length between the tenons as the lower rails.

1. Start by tenoning one end of each upper end-rail blank. Note that the finished tenon must be offset so that it is just above the bottom edge of the rail blank.

2. Use a lower end rail to scribe the opposite shoulder of the upper end-rail tenon. Using one rail to mark out the other is both easier and more accurate than measuring.

3. Cut and fit the remaining tenons.

4. Now mark out the upper curve of the rail, using a thin strip of wood as shown (see **Photo C**).

5. Cut the curve on the bandsaw and smooth with either a plane (you really can plane a convex curve like this, but you have to get the feel of keeping the cutting edge on the wood as you work the curve) or sandpaper. A piece of the offcut makes a great sanding block for smoothing out a curve.

6. Use a marking gauge (I attached a pencil to a cheap marking gauge for just this purpose—see **Photo D** on p. 40) to mark the lower curve parallel to the upper one. (See "A Homemade Marking Gauge" for an alternate device.) Bandsaw and smooth the lower curve.

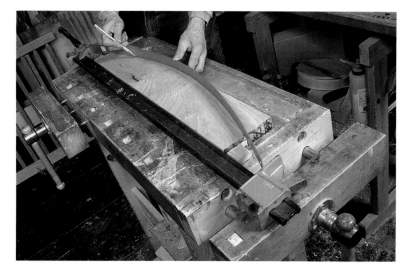

PHOTO C: Springing a 3-ft. ruler or a thin strip of wood with a clamp is an easy way to lay out a curve. Adjust the curve by tightening or loosening the clamp until you have the curve you want.

A Homemade Marking Gauge

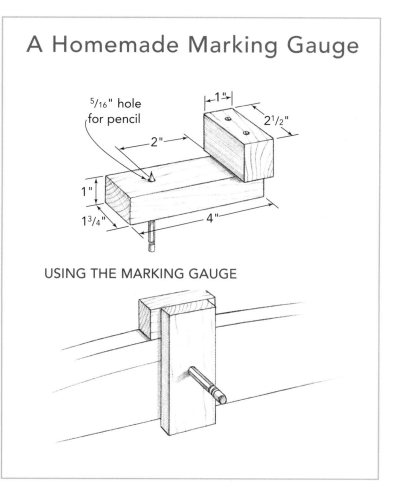

USING THE MARKING GAUGE

PHOTO D: A marking gauge locates the bottom of the upper end rail from the curve of the top.

PHOTO E: Dowel points transfer the exact locations of the holes in the end of the inner front rail to the inside of the lower end rail.

Making the lower back rail

1. Drill ⅜-in. holes for the bolts in both ends of the lower back rail. Use a self-centering dowel jig set up to drill the hole in the middle of the 5-in.-wide rail. The hole should be 4 in. deep. Drill as deep as you can with the jig in place; then remove the jig and deepen the hole, if necessary.

2. If you used the alignment-pin jig for the alignment-pin holes in the legs, drill the dowel holes in the ends of the rail with the same jig. These holes should be about 1 in. deep. Otherwise, mark the hole locations with dowel centers and drill with the self-centering dowel jig.

3. Make a recess for the washer and nut on each end of the inside face of the rail by drilling with a 1-in. or 1¼-in. Forstner bit, centered 4⅜ in. from the end. The holes should be ¹⁵⁄₁₆ in. deep, but check before you drill to make sure the point of the drill won't come through to the outside of the rail. Forstner bits typically have very short points and are ideal for this type of hole.

4. Use a chisel to square up the side of the holes closest to the ends.

5. Glue the alignment pins—⁵⁄₁₆-in. by 1¼-in. dowels—into the ⁵⁄₁₆-in. holes in both ends of the rail.

Making the inner front rail

The inner front rail needs to be behind the front legs to allow the front gate to slide down. It attaches to the inside face of the end rails the same way the back rail attaches to the back legs.

1. Start by dry-assembling the two lower end rails with the back legs.

2. Bolt on the lower back rail one side at a time by inserting the alignment pins on the end of the rail into the dowel holes in the leg. Insert a ⁵⁄₁₆-in. by 5½-in. hex-head bolt with a washer through the counterbored hole in the outside of the leg and place a washer and then a nut onto the end of the bolt in the nut recess in the rail. Tighten the bolt with a nut driver or socket wrench, holding the nut with a wrench.

3. Measure the distance between the two end rails at the back legs. This is the length of the inner front rail.

4. Cut the inner front rail to length.

5. Drill both ends of the lower front rail for the bolt and alignment pins just as you did for the lower back rail. Drill and chisel the nut recess as well. The only difference is that the rail is narrower. The bolt hole should be centered on the inner front rail, but it will be lower than center on the end rail, because the bottom edges of these two rails align.

6. Now mark out the location for the bolt and alignment-pin holes in the lower end rails by using dowel points (see **Photo E**).

7. You can drill the two ⁵⁄₁₆-in. alignment-pin holes ½ in. deep, but measure the location of the central bolt hole and then transfer that location around to the outside of the end rail.

8. Start on the outside of the end rail and drill a ¾-in. counterbore for the bolt head. This should be ⅜ in. deep.

9. Now drill the ⅜-in. bolt hole from the inside of the rail, guided by the mark from the dowel pin.

Making the upper rails

The upper back rail has two short tenons that fit into the mortises at the tops of the back legs. These tenons do not get glued into place; the bolts on the lower back rail will hold them in. The upper back rail between the shoulders is exactly the same length as the lower back rail between the shoulders. The upper front rail is ¹⁄₃₂ in. shorter, because it needs to slide freely up and down between the legs.

1. Cut both of the rails to width.

2. Cut the upper front rail to ¹⁄₃₂ in. less than the distance between the shoulders on the lower back rail (which should be equal to the distance between the front legs as well). Set aside any extra length; you'll need it later for testing the drop gate.

3. Cut the upper back rail to 1 in. longer than the distance between the shoulders on the lower back rail to allow for the ½-in.-long tenons on either end.

4. Cut the ½-in. by 1½-in. by ½-in.-long tenons on both ends of the upper back rail.

Making the lower front rail

Cut the lower front (gate) rail to exactly the same length as the upper front (gate) rail. That's all you need to do with this rail for right now.

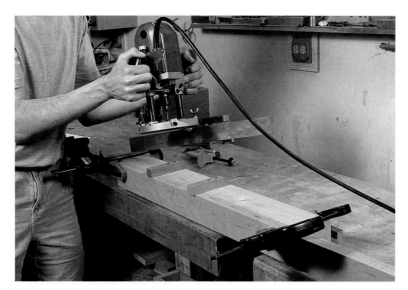

PHOTO F: Mortising the rails for all of the slats can go quickly if you make stops for the mortising-block jig. Align the layout marks on the rail with marks on the jig to set up for each mortise.

Cutting the mortises in the front and back rails

1. Mark out the locations for the slat mortises on the upper edge of the lower back rail; then clamp it together with the upper back rail, aligning the tenon edges. Transfer the marks. Be sure to mark the lower edge of the rail.

2. Clamp the lower front rail to the lower back rail, centering the front rail between the tenons on the back rail. Transfer the mortise locations. Then clamp the upper front rail to the lower and transfer the mortise locations.

3. I mortised the rails using the mortising jig shown in "Mortising Block" on p. 12. I made marks on the jig to line up with the mortise marks on the rails and screwed stops to the top of the mortising jig to limit the travel of the router to exactly the desired mortise size (see **Photo F**).

Making the Slats

This is the part of the job that most people dread. But with some careful planning and setup, it's not that bad.

PHOTO G: If you set up carefully, cutting all of the slat tenons can go quickly and accurately.

Milling the slats

1. Start by milling the stock for the slats to 1 in. thick. You will rip ⅜-in. strips from this wood. Calculate to be sure you have enough for all 32 slats, plus 4 or 5 extra. Cut the stock to length now (including tenon lengths).

2. Before you do anything else, plane or sand the faces of these boards smooth. This will save a lot of time smoothing out edges on individual slats later on.

3. Now rip the slats to width. Be sure to use a push stick. If you find an edge is no longer straight, rejoint that edge before continuing.

Tenoning the slats

1. I cut the ¼-in. by ¾-in. by ⅜-in.-long slat tenons on the table saw, using a plywood sliding table with a stop attached to the front fence (see **Photo G**). Take your time and set up for cutting the tenons very carefully. Use an extra slat to test out your setup, so you have as little hand fitting as possible.

2. Test-fit all of the tenons in their mortises. You don't want any surprises when you go to glue up an assembly with this many parts. Adjust the tenons, if necessary, for a fit that is snug but not too tight to insert with some effort by hand. Loose tenons should be patched and refit.

Making the Slat Assemblies

As with most complex assemblies, things go easier if you prepare everything beforehand and proceed methodically.

Preparing the parts for assembly

1. Smooth the remaining faces of the slats.
2. Chamfer the edges of the slats. I used a router table with a fence and a 45-degree chamfer bit. Then smooth the chamfers with a few swipes with 220-grit sandpaper.
3. Smooth out all of the rail faces and edges.
4. Rout, plane, or sand a ⅟₁₆-in. chamfer on all edges of the lower rails.
5. Round over all of the edges on the upper rails using a ⅛-in. roundover bit mounted in a router.

Assembling the slats and rails

The key to putting the slats and rails together is to work on one slat at a time. This is easier than it sounds. Repeat these procedures for both the stationary back and front drop-gate assemblies.

1. Get together everything you'll need for your glue-up: clamps with clamp pads, glue, a small stick for spreading the glue in the mortises, a tape measure to check for square, a security blanket, and whatever else you feel you need.

2. Clamp the lower rail onto a workbench and spread glue in all of the mortises. You should just wet the sides of the mortises. Don't apply so much that you have glue pooling at the bottoms.

3. Working quickly and steadily, insert each slat into place. Pound down if necessary with a non-marring mallet.

4. Now spread glue in the upper rail mortises.

5. Start at one end and fit the tenon of the first slat into its mortise. Push or tap down gently. Keep the other end of the rail up.

6. When the first tenon is positioned just inside the rim of its mortise, work the next slat tenon into its mortise. Push or tap down. Keep the upper rail angled, so you are working on just one or two slats at a time.

Put a clamp on the end you started with, if necessary, to keep the angle. Work your way across to the other side of the rail as shown (see **Photo H**).

7. Place three or four clamps on alternate sides of the slat-and-rail assembly and tighten evenly until the joints are all the way home.

8. As a safety measure, all of the slats should be pinned in place. There are a couple of ways to do this. If you have access to a pin nailer (a pneumatic or electric nail gun for small pins or wire brads), you can simply shoot pins into the rails in the appropriate places so they secure the tenons as well. Or you can drill holes and pin with thin wooden dowels.

PHOTO H: Starting at one side and working across makes assembly a one-person job. I use a non-marring rubber mallet to tap each slat into its mortise.

Making the End Panels

1. Mill the wood for the two end panels to ½ in. thick; then joint and glue the individual boards into panels that are at least 28¼ in. wide by 26½ in. long.

2. Plane and sand the panels flat and smooth.

Cutting the grooves for the end panels

It's a good idea to start with the grooves in the upper and lower rails—it's easier to adjust the grooves in the legs to match if you have to.

1. Rout the ½-in.-wide by ½-in.-deep groove in each upper end rail with a slotting cutter. You'll have to set up the rail on top of a scrap of plywood (cut roughly to shape) to leave room for the bearing. You should also set up a support for the router a couple inches away from the rail you're cutting. I used the other rail (see **Photo I**). Just be careful not to rout into it. You'll have to take two or three passes to cut the groove wide enough. Start with the router set to cut higher up; then lower it on subsequent passes. This way you won't rout away your bearing surface. End the groove at full depth at the shoulder of the tenons; don't cut all the way through to the end of the tenon.

PHOTO I: The upper end rails must be clamped in place before you start routing. You'll have to stop and move the clamps to complete the groove.

2. Cut the groove in each of the lower rails with the router and slotting cutter (you won't need the fancy setup) or on the table saw. This groove should also be ½ in. by ½ in.

3. Dry-fit the rails into the legs and mark out the locations for the grooves on the legs. If all is well, they will line up perfectly. Rout the ½-in.-wide by ⅜-in.-deep grooves in the legs with a router and fence using a straight bit. If the grooves do not line up, you can

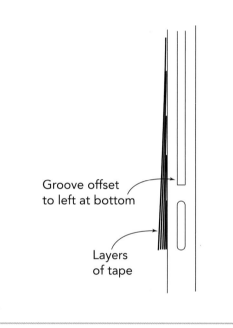
use a little trick I came up with, shown in "Routing Misaligned Panel Grooves."
4. Chisel the bottom ends of the leg grooves square.

Cutting the end panels to shape

Start the process of cutting the panels by once again dry-fitting the legs and rails together. Check that the grooves all line up. You can adjust the grooves if necessary by sanding the appropriate side of a groove with sandpaper on a thin piece of wood.

Check too that the leg grooves extend all the way down to the bottom of the rail grooves. Mark and remove more wood if necessary. Do this for both of the end assemblies.
1. Measure the overall width of the panel opening (bottom of groove to bottom of groove). This should be 1¼ in. more than the distance between the legs. Subtract ½ in. to get the panel width. This will allow for expansion and contraction. Rip the panel to this width.
2. Measure the overall height at the center of the rails (bottom of groove to bottom of groove). The panel should be about ³⁄₁₆ in. shorter than this measure. Cut the bottom of the panel square; then measure up and mark this distance at the center of the panel.
3. Use the bottom edge of the other upper end rail to mark out the curve on the top of the panel. Measure up from the bottom at both sides of the panel to be sure the ends of the upper rail are equidistant from the bottom before marking the curve. Cut to shape.

Fitting the panels

Follow these procedures for each of the end assemblies.
1. Start by fitting the first panel to the lower and upper end rails. Sand or plane the edges of the panel until it fits into the grooves. Then move on to fitting to the grooves in the legs.
2. When all four sides of the panel fit into the proper grooves, check the overall fit by dry-assembling the panel with the rails and legs.
3. The panel should fit all the way to the bottom of the lower rail groove, leaving all of the space at the top. When you are sure that everything fits together properly, carefully disassemble the crib end.

Gluing Up the End Assemblies

Planning and preparation ensure that the glue-ups will go smoothly (or at least more smoothly than they would otherwise).

1. Get together all of the clamps, pads, glue, and whatever else you need.

2. Slip the upper and lower end rails onto the panel, without using any glue.

3. Spread glue in the mortises in the legs and then very lightly on the tenons.

4. Insert the tenons into the mortises; push together; and clamp, using appropriate pads to protect the work.

5. Don't use too much pressure on the upper end rail. You may want to add a clamp from the upper rail down to the lower rail to keep the upper rail from flexing up under the pressure. This should help seat the tenon thoroughly.

6. If you want to attach fabric-covered bumpers to the inside of the crib (check with the parents-to-be), you should drill holes now for the ties that will attach them to the legs.

Installing the Front Drop-Gate Hardware

The front drop gate on the crib slides on metal guide pins mounted in holes drilled in the ends of the rails. These pins slide in the grooves in the legs. I cut the pins out of ¼-in. steel rod that I picked up at the hardware store.

1. Mark a line 1 in. up from the bottom of the lower front rail and align a self-centering dowel jig so the ¼-in. hole is centered on this line.

2. Drill the ¼-in. hole about 1½ in. deep. Repeat for the other end of the rail.

3. The upper front rail is more complicated. The hole needs to be located so that the rail is centered on the leg and is about ⅟₁₆ in. down from the top when the pin is in place in the bottom of the shepherd's-hook groove. Take the scrap piece of front rail you saved earlier (or mill up a new piece exactly the same size) and hold it up in the proper location. Make sure it covers all of the hook groove. Trace the location onto the leg.

4. Now measure for the location of the guide pin. Find the distance from both the outside and the bottom edge of the rail to the pin location at the bottom of the shep-

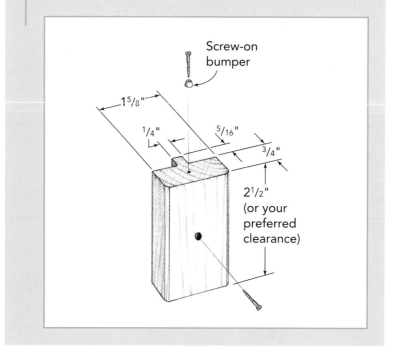
herd's hook. It's easier to measure to the edges of the groove and then to find the center by adding ⅛ in.

5. Mark out the center of the pin location on the end of your scrap. To drill the hole off center, you'll need to make up a spacer to clamp in the self-centering dowel jig with the rail groove (see "Drilling for the Drop-Gate Pins" on p. 46). This will offset the jig the proper amount.

6. Set up the dowel jig with the spacer on the inside face of the scrap piece. Align the jig with your pin-location mark; then drill. Insert a short length of metal rod into the hole and check the location of the scrap piece on the leg when the metal rod is in the shepherd's-hook groove.

Drilling for the Drop-Gate Pins

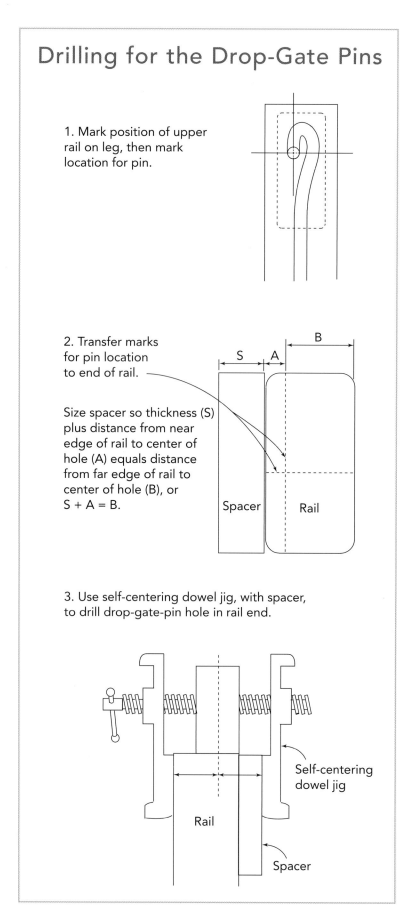

1. Mark position of upper rail on leg, then mark location for pin.

2. Transfer marks for pin location to end of rail.

Size spacer so thickness (S) plus distance from near edge of rail to center of hole (A) equals distance from far edge of rail to center of hole (B), or S + A = B.

B

S A

Spacer Rail

3. Use self-centering dowel jig, with spacer, to drill drop-gate-pin hole in rail end.

Self-centering dowel jig

Rail

Spacer

7. Make any necessary corrections (and check again); then drill the upper rail ends.
8. Cut the pins to 1¾ in. long, file the ends smooth, and ease the edges.
9. Put a very small amount of epoxy in the holes; then tap the pins into place, until just under ⁵⁄₁₆ in. remains protruding.

Setting Up the Crib

It's a good idea to set up the crib now to test out the fit and the workings of the drop gate. You can make any necessary adjustments before the finish goes on.
1. Bolt the back-rail assembly into place on one end of the crib and tighten.
2. Bolt the other end onto the back rail.
3. Add the inner front rail, gently spreading the ends apart to make room; then bolt into place.
4. Tip the crib onto its back. Take the front gate and slide the upper rail pins into the slot in the legs (see **Photo J**).
5. Continue carefully until you can insert the lower rail pins. Slide the gate all the way up, then lift the crib up onto all four legs.

PHOTO J: Slide the front drop gate up the groove in the front legs.

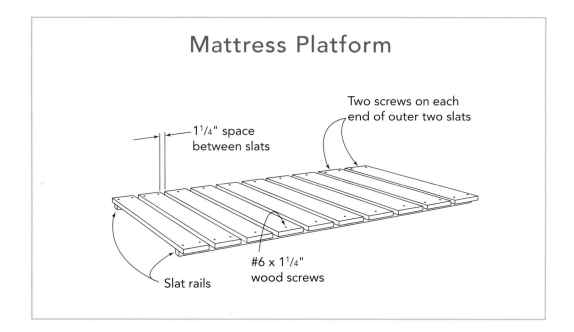

Mattress Platform

1¼" space between slats

Two screws on each end of outer two slats

#6 x 1¼" wood screws

Slat rails

Making the Mattress Platform

1. Make up a support cleat for the mattress platform 1 in. by 1¼ in. by 51¼ in. long. Drill a series of pilot holes for screws to attach the cleat to the lower back rail.

2. Scribe a line 4 in. from the bottom of this rail on the inside of the crib. Line up the top edge of the cleat with the line and screw into place.

3. Make up the platform out of 10 slats, ¾ in. thick and 4 in. wide, with two rails screwed underneath (see "Mattress Platform"). It is best if the slat rails are positioned so that when the assembly is installed, the rails are adjacent to the support cleat at the back and to the inner front rail at the front. That's just over 1⅛ in. from the front edge

of the slats and just over 1 in. from the back edge.

4. Secure the mattress platform to the crib frame with one screw in each corner, through the slats and into the inner front rail and the cleat in the back.

Finishing

When choosing a finish, remember that infants and toddlers tend to gnaw on things like the upper rails of a crib. And whatever finish you choose, be sure to allow enough time so it can cure completely before you put the crib into use.

If desired, screw the rubber bumpers to the underside of the lower front gate rail, and you're finished.

CHILD'S FOUR-POSTER BED

THIS IS A BED THAT GETS a lot of attention. People tend to ooh and ah over the toddler-size version of this four-poster—made for a standard crib-size mattress—more than over almost any other bed I've made (for child or adult). This project is great fun, but there is a very practical side to the design as well. Kids really like a bed that is not too big for them, especially when they're just moving from their crib. And when the time comes for a more adult-size bed, it's not that hard to make up new rails and a new headboard to convert the bed to fit a regular twin mattress; most of the work goes into the posts, and they stay the same.

I originally built this bed for my daughter after she began climbing out of her crib. She loved it, so I expanded the bed for her when she started to outgrow it. She now keeps interesting hats hanging on all four posts. Of course, you can make the bed in a twin size (or any other size) right from the start, for either a toddler or an older child of any age.

CHILD'S FOUR-POSTER BED

THIS FOUR-POSTER BED, sized for a crib mattress, bolts together. None of the joints is glued, so the bed can be dismantled for both storage and moving. Note the offset bolt holes through the posts, which allow you to attach both the side rails and the headboard and footboard rails.

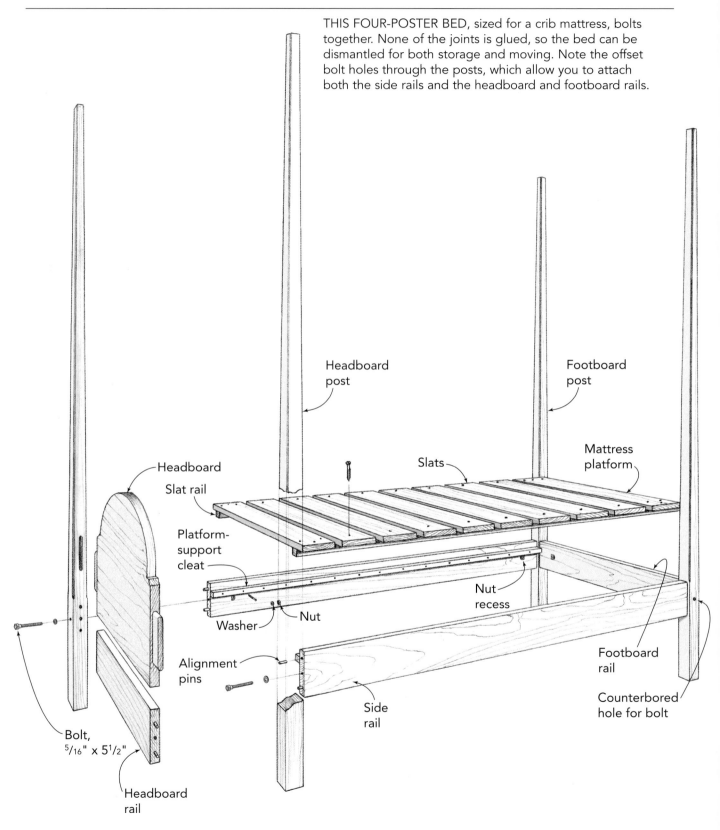

Headboard post

Footboard post

Headboard

Slat rail

Slats

Mattress platform

Platform-support cleat

Nut recess

Washer

Nut

Alignment pins

Footboard rail

Side rail

Counterbored hole for bolt

Bolt, ⁵⁄₁₆" x 5¹⁄₂"

Headboard rail

FRONT VIEW

SIDE VIEW

TOP OF POST

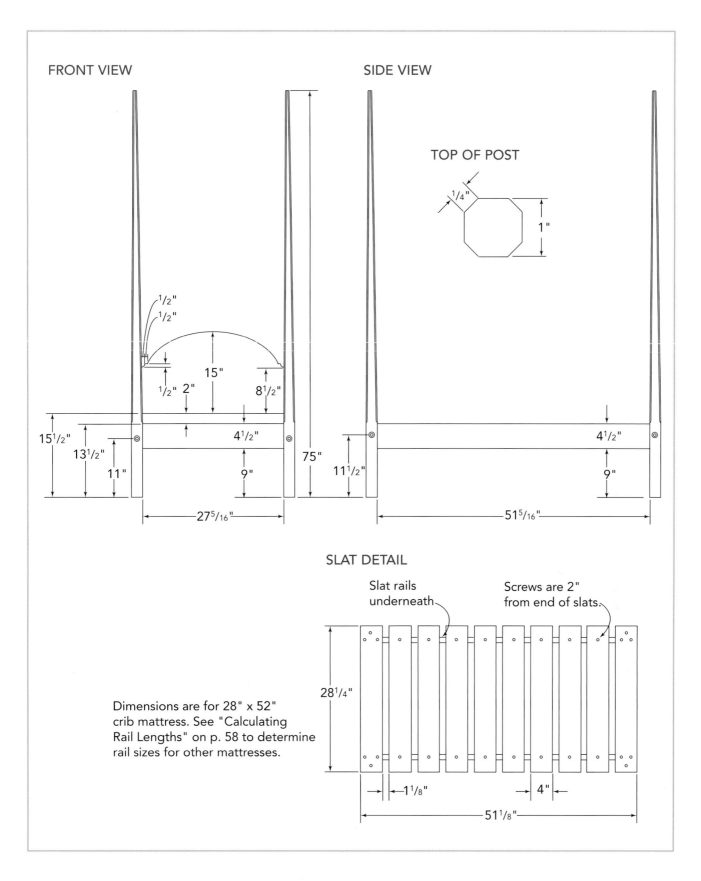

1/2"
1/2"
15"
1/2" 2"
8 1/2"
4 1/2"
15 1/2"
13 1/2"
11"
9"
75"
27 5/16"

11 1/2"
4 1/2"
9"
51 5/16"

1/4"
1"

SLAT DETAIL

Slat rails
underneath

Screws are 2"
from end of slats

28 1/4"

Dimensions are for 28" x 52"
crib mattress. See "Calculating
Rail Lengths" on p. 58 to determine
rail sizes for other mattresses.

1 1/8"
4"
51 1/8"

CUT LIST FOR CHILD'S FOUR-POSTER BED

4	Posts	2" x 2" x 75"
2	Rails (1 headboard and 1 footboard)	1¹⁄₁₆" x 4½" x 27⁵⁄₁₆"
2	Side rails	1¹⁄₁₆" x 4½" x 51⁵⁄₁₆"
1	Headboard panel	1¹⁄₁₆" x 16" x 28⅜"*
2	Cleats	1" x 1¼" x 51"
10	Slats	¾" x 4" x 28¼"
2	Slat rails	¾" x 1¼" x 51"
Hardware		
8	Bolts with nuts	8⁵⁄₁₆" x 5½"
16	Washers	⁵⁄₁₆" SAE**
16	Dowels (for alignment pins)	⁵⁄₁₆" x 1¼"

*Including the tenons.
**These have a slightly larger hole than standard ⁵⁄₁₆" washers. Most hardware stores and auto parts stores carry them.

THE BULK OF THE WORK on the four-poster bed goes into making the posts: shaping the long tapers and drilling for the bed-rail joinery. After that, the rails are quite easy. You return to a challenge when making the headboard, which has both interesting joinery and some nice curves to shape.

Making the Parts

Sizing and marking the posts

It is very important that you realize that the four posts are all different (though symmetrical) and are not interchangeable. The most difficult part of this project is keeping track of the different offset hole locations on each of the four posts. Mark these out very carefully and then double-check everything by arranging the posts as they will be on the bed and verifying that the layout at each location is correct. Only then should you start to drill. I have to confess that I messed up one of the posts while prototyping the bed and drilled the countersunk hole on the inside. Luckily, I was able to salvage the post

Post Joinery

Each post is unique; label the posts on either top or bottom so you don't get them mixed up.

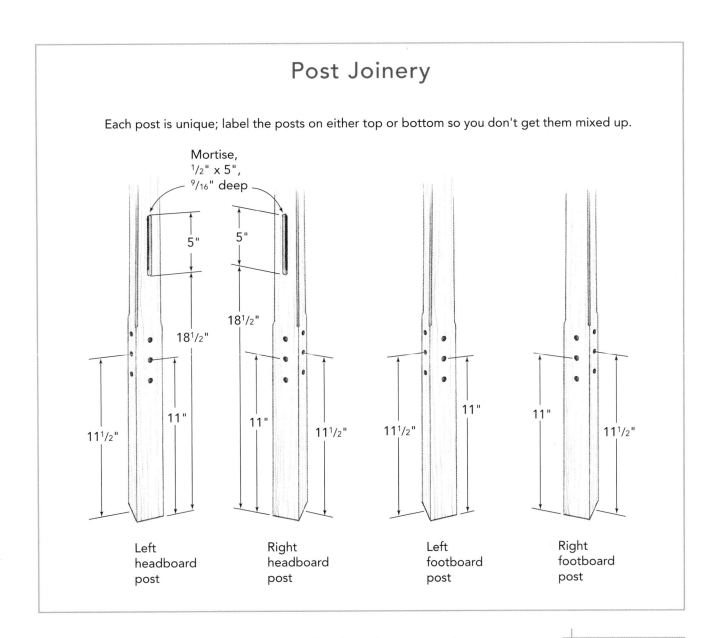

Mortise,
$1/2$" x 5",
$9/16$" deep

5"   5"

$18^1/_2$" $18^1/_2$"

$11^1/_2$"   11"   11" $11^1/_2$" $11^1/_2$"   11"   11" $11^1/_2$"

Left
headboard
post

Right
headboard
post

Left
footboard
post

Right
footboard
post

because it was the first one I drilled; I shifted it to another location.

1. Mill the wood for the posts to 2 in. square. Then cut all four posts to 75 in. long.

2. Arrange the posts the way you would like them, paying attention to the appearance of the grain. Remember that you will be tapering the posts so some superficial defects can be removed as you taper.

3. Careful layout and marking are critical. Lay out and mark the locations for the rails and for each of the holes in each post (see "Post Joinery"). Mark the hole locations carefully on both inside and outside faces of the posts. Check your layout meticulously.

Cutting the post joinery and tapering

1. Start by drilling the ⅞-in. counterbores for the bolt heads ⁵⁄₁₆ in. deep. Then drill down through the center of the counterbore with a ⅜-in. drill about halfway through the post. Then drill back through from the inside of the post until the holes meet up. This way, the holes will be centered on both the inside and the outside of the posts. I used a fence and a stop on the drill press to help with this process. Be sure to move the stop when you change from the holes for the side rails to the holes for the headboard and footboard (see **Photo A** on p. 54).

TIP
Before you get them down to the exact size, it pays to check that the posts are indeed square.

PHOTO A: Drill the bolt holes through the posts carefully on the drill press. Drill from both sides to ensure that the hole is centered on the inside and outside faces.

2. Use a specially made jig to drill the holes for the alignment pins (see **Photos B** and **C** and "Alignment-Pin Jig" on p. 15). When positioning the jig, measure carefully to be sure that it is (and therefore the holes will be) parallel to the sides of the post. Drill the alignment-pin holes about ½ in. deep.

3. Lay out the locations for the headboard mortises and cut them ⁹⁄₁₆ in. deep using a plunge router with a fence. I stopped the cuts when I came to the layout lines, although you can clamp stops in place if you choose (see **Photo D**).

4. Mark out the tops of each of the posts with a marking gauge set to ½ in. (see **Photo E**). This will give you layout lines for the final size (1 in. square) of the top of each post.

5. Mark the posts where the tapers begin, 14 in. above the bottoms. Mark out the tapers by connecting these points with the

TIP
Make several very shallow passes when using a plunge router to cut mortises, rather than one full-depth pass. You'll get cleaner, more accurate results.

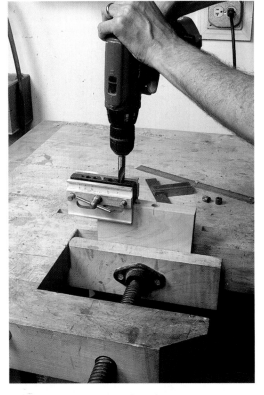

PHOTO B: To make the alignment-pin jig, carefully mark out an oversize block of wood, and then drill using a self-centering dowel jig. Cut the jig to size.

PHOTO C: Clamp the alignment-pin jig in place, parallel with the sides of the post, and drill the holes about ½ in. deep.

layout lines at the top of the post. You need to do this on only one post if you're cutting the tapers on the table saw with the jig shown in "The Tapering Jig" on p. 56.

6. Cut the tapers on all four legs as shown (see **Photo F**).

7. Smooth the posts by a combination of planing, scraping, and sanding that works for you. Be careful that the areas where the rails attach are flat (not tapered) and square. But don't worry about keeping a defined line where the tapers begin; it's actually better to have that transition blurred a little.

8. The posts are chamfered along each of the corners above the rails (see **Photo G**). But before routing them, mark out the headboard plank from the assembled posts and rail. Make the chamfers about ¼ in. wide. The chamfers should start about 13½ in. up from the bottom of the post (even with the top of the rails). You can use a very simple jig to help place the start of the chamfer for each of the four corners in exactly the same place (see "A Jig to Locate Stopped Cham-

PHOTO D: Clamp the post to the bench before routing the headboard mortise. Use a second leg, also clamped to the bench, to help support the router during the cuts.

PHOTO E: Marking the top of the posts for tapering is quick and accurate if you use a marking gauge.

TIP
Save the cut-off wedges from the two mortised faces of the headboard posts. These wedges will make it easier to cut the ends of the headboard plank to the proper angle.

PHOTO F: When tapering the posts on a table saw, you'll need an outfeed roller or an assistant to support the long posts with jig as they leave the saw.

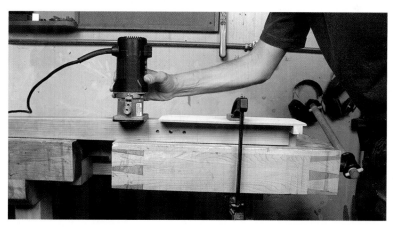

PHOTO G: The chamfer stop hooks over the bottom end of the post. The router stops chamfering when its base contacts the end of the jig.

THE TAPERING JIG

It takes two setups to cut a four-sided taper. You can set up for the first cuts on each post and then move the alignment blocks for the second set of cuts. Or you can make two different jigs. The alignment blocks also work as part of the hold-down for securing the post during the cuts.

Tighten the screw on the wooden hold-down to hold the post to the base. Loosen the screw to unclamp the post. Set the top alignment block so the top of the post overhangs the jig base by about ½ in. Set the bottom alignment block so that the lower 14 in. of the post does *not* overhang the jig base (and so will not be cut).

Alternatively, you can cut the tapers on a bandsaw. Mark the tapers on one face of each post and bandsaw the two sides. Rotate the post 90 degrees and mark out the tapers on one of the band-sawn faces; then cut the remaining two tapers. Be sure to mark the tapers starting a little higher up on the post—about 15 in.—to allow room for smoothing.

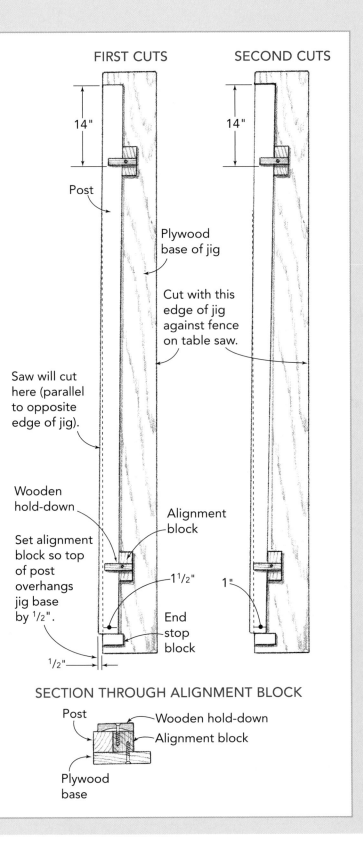

FIRST CUTS   SECOND CUTS

14"

14"

Post

Plywood base of jig

Cut with this edge of jig against fence on table saw.

Saw will cut here (parallel to opposite edge of jig).

Wooden hold-down

Set alignment block so top of post overhangs jig base by ½".

Alignment block

1½"

1"

End stop block

½"

SECTION THROUGH ALIGNMENT BLOCK

Post

Wooden hold-down

Alignment block

Plywood base

A Jig to Locate Stopped Chamfers

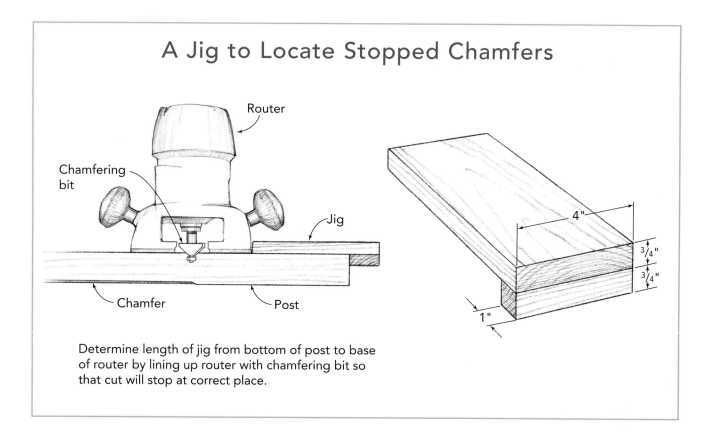

Router

Chamfering bit

Jig

Chamfer

Post

4"

3/4"

3/4"

1"

Determine length of jig from bottom of post to base of router by lining up router with chamfering bit so that cut will stop at correct place.

fers"). Smooth the chamfers; then ease or lightly chamfer the top and bottom edges of each post.

Making the rails

1. Mill the wood to 1¹⁄₁₆ in. thick and rip to 4½ in. wide. You can cut the rails to the lengths given in the cut list if all of your rails and posts are the specified thickness. If any of the dimensions are off, or if you are making a different size bed, you should calculate the exact lengths (see "Calculating Rail Lengths" on p. 58).

2. Lay out the locations for the bolt holes in the rails. These are offset from center just as the holes in the posts are offset. The bolt holes in the side rails are 2 in. up from the bottom of the rails and those on the headboard and footboard rails are 2½ in. up. Mark the inside faces of the rails, and extend your marks 4 in. down these faces (see "Rail Joinery").

3. Drill the bolt holes with a ⅜-in. drill bit, using a self-centering dowel jig. Align the jig carefully with the marks. The holes should be about 4 in. deep.

Rail Joinery

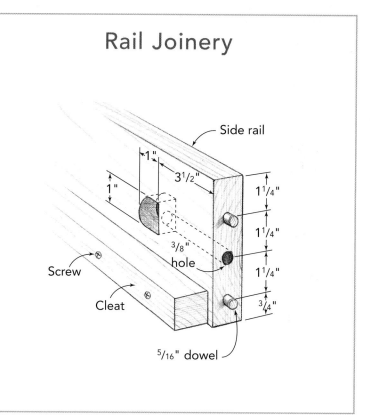

Side rail

1"

3½"

1"

1¼"

1¼"

3/8" hole

1¼"

Screw

Cleat

3/4"

5/16" dowel

CALCULATING RAIL LENGTHS

The length of the rails on a bed depends on several factors: mattress size, desired clearance around the mattress (approximately ¼ in. is good for a child's bed), rail thickness, and post thickness. The easiest way to understand the way the different variables work is to make a simple section drawing at the rail height.

All of the math can be reduced to a fairly simple formula:

rail length = (mattress dimension + clearance) - (post thickness - rail thickness)

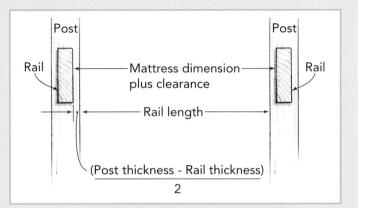

This formula will work for any size bed you wish to build. Note that for other beds, you may have to factor in the length of the tenons on the ends of the rails, which isn't necessary here.

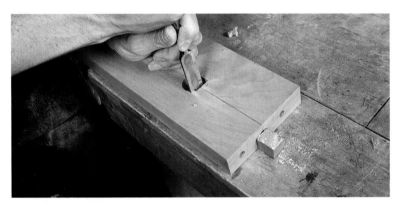

PHOTO H: Pare the end of the recess for the nut flat and smooth. Multiple small cuts usually give you more control and a better end result than chopping the flat all at once.

4. Drill the alignment-pin holes, using a custom drilling jig (see "Alignment-Pin Jig" on p. 15). Make sure the edge of the jig is parallel to the rail before clamping the jig and beginning to drill. These holes should be deep enough to allow ⅜ in. of the dowels to protrude when you insert them.

5. Drill holes for the nuts and washers on the inside face of each rail. The holes should be centered on the marks you made for the bolt holes, 4 in. from the end of the rail. Use a 1-in. or 1¼-in. Forstner bit so you can drill to within about 3/16 in. of the outside face of the rail. Don't let the point come through.

6. Chisel a flat at the side of each hole closest to the end if the rail (see **Photo H**). If the chisel is sharp and you pare away the wood little at a time, the results will be cleaner than if you chop away the wood in a hurry.

7. Glue 5/16-in. dowel pins into the holes; then cut them off, if necessary, so you have about ⅜ in. extending out from the end of the rail. Chamfer the ends of the pins with a pencil sharpener or sandpaper.

8. Chamfer all four edges of the headboard and footboard rails, and both upper edges and the outside bottom edge of the side rails. Check to be sure you have the rails oriented properly, with the bolt holes closer to the bottom, before you chamfer.

Making the headboard

Although the headboard has two tenons, it does not get glued into place. Instead, the

Headboard Details

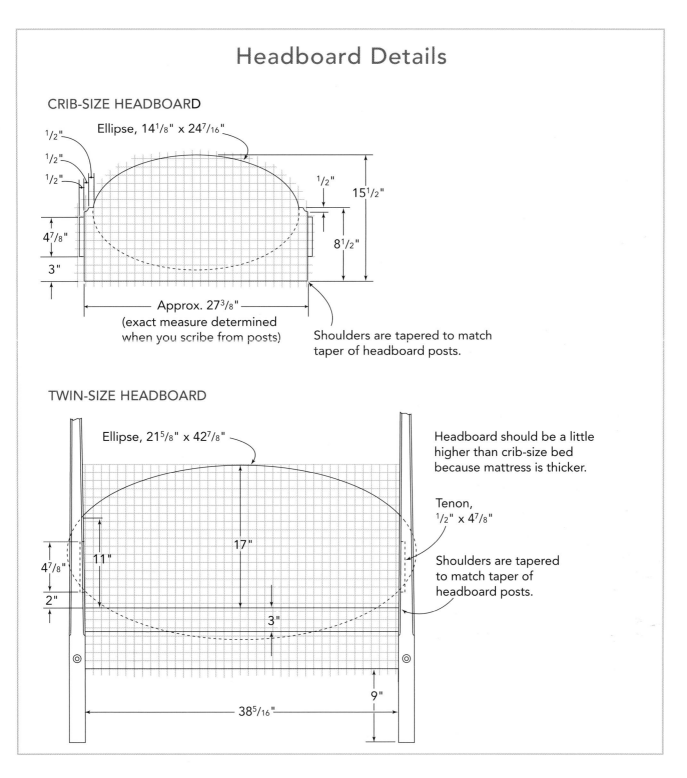

CRIB-SIZE HEADBOARD

Ellipse, $14^{1}/_{8}$" x $24^{7}/_{16}$"

$^{1}/_{2}$"
$^{1}/_{2}$"
$^{1}/_{2}$"

$^{1}/_{2}$"

$15^{1}/_{2}$"

$4^{7}/_{8}$"

$8^{1}/_{2}$"

3"

Approx. $27^{3}/_{8}$"
(exact measure determined
when you scribe from posts)

Shoulders are tapered to match
taper of headboard posts.

TWIN-SIZE HEADBOARD

Ellipse, $21^{5}/_{8}$" x $42^{7}/_{8}$"

Headboard should be a little
higher than crib-size bed
because mattress is thicker.

Tenon,
$^{1}/_{2}$" x $4^{7}/_{8}$"

Shoulders are tapered
to match taper of
headboard posts.

17"

11"

$4^{7}/_{8}$"

2"

3"

9"

$38^{5}/_{16}$"

tenons are loose in the mortises in the posts, and the headboard is held in place by the bolted headboard rail. Note that the headboard ends are not parallel; the tenon shoulders follow the taper of the posts (see "Headboard Details" above and "Cutting the Headboard Tenons" on p. 60).

1. First glue up the blank for the headboard out of $1^{1}/_{16}$-in.-thick stock. The blank should be just over 16 in. wide by 28 in. long.
2. Smooth the blank on both sides, planing, scraping, and/or sanding so it is flat and smooth.

Cutting the Headboard Tenons

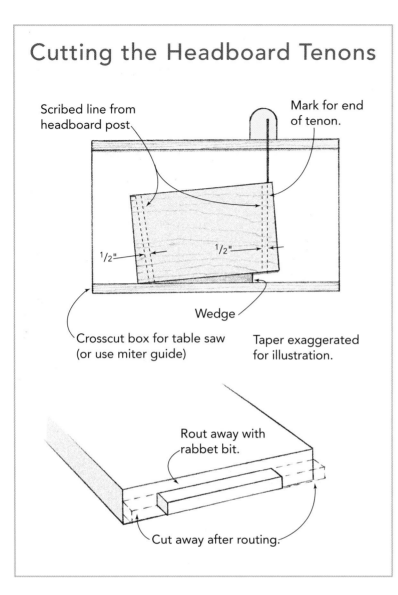

Scribed line from headboard post.

Mark for end of tenon.

1/2" 1/2"

Wedge

Crosscut box for table saw (or use miter guide)

Taper exaggerated for illustration.

Rout away with rabbet bit.

Cut away after routing.

3. Check to be sure that you have one good straight edge. If not, joint an edge smooth and straight. Rip the opposite edge parallel, making the blank 15½ in. wide.

4. Assemble the headboard posts with the headboard rail and tighten the bolts. Lay the headboard blank down and place the post-and-rail assembly over it. Make up two 2-in.-long spacer blocks and use them to position the bottom edge of the blank parallel to and 2 in. from the top edge of the rail. Mark the shoulders of the headboard blank by tracing the inside faces of the posts onto it (see **Photo I**).

5. Carefully mark out the ends of the blank (the ends of the tenons) exactly ½ in. to the outside of the scribed shoulder lines.

6. Cut the ends of the blank, using the off-cut wedges from tapering the two faces of the headboard post to help you get the exact angle (see "Cutting the Headboard Tenons"). Cut outside the line first and adjust the angle, if necessary.

7. Cut the tenons on the ends of the plank by routing with a ½-in. rabbet bit on both sides of each end. Set the depth of cut so you leave a tenon of the correct thickness—or preferably just a little over (see **Photo J**).

8. Fit the tenon to the mortise in the headboard rails by planing with a cheek or rabbet plane or by sanding or filing.

9. Cut the top of the headboard to shape.

PHOTO I: To scribe the shoulders of the headboard, place the headboard blank over the headboard post-and-rail assembly. Note the spacer blocks, which help position the headboard the proper distance from the top edge of headboard rail.

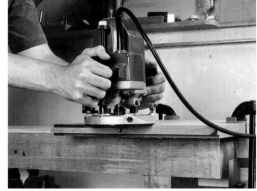

PHOTO J: Mark out the thickness of the tenon on the end of the headboard; then rout with a ½-in. rabbet bit from both faces of the headboard.

10. The small curves can be smoothed with a small drum sander mounted on a drill press or by hand with a dowel wrapped with sandpaper. A sanding block works well for the larger curve.

Making the platform parts

1. Mill the two platform-support cleats to 1 in. by 1¼ in. by 51 in. long.

2. Drill pilot holes for the screws you'll use to attach the cleat to the rails.

3. The cleats attach flush to the bottom inside edge of the two side rails. (This edge of the rails is not chamfered.) Attach the cleats with #6 by 1¼-in. screws. I usually leave the cleats unfinished and attach them after I have completely finished the rails.

4. Mill up enough soft maple for 10 slats, ¾ in. thick by 1¼ in. wide. Cut one to 28¼ in. long and check the fit between the rails. Then cut the rest.

5. Cut two slat rails to size, ¾ in. by 1¼ in. by 51 in. long

6. Drill pilot holes in the slats 2 in. from each end, lay out the slats on the assembled bed, spaced as shown on p. 51. Clamp the two slat rails in place below the slats. Then screw the slats down into the slat rails.

Assembling the Bed

The next step is to assemble the bed. Involve your child in the project if you think he or she will be interested.

1. Assemble the headboard section first. Attach one of the headboard posts to the headboard rail with a ⁵⁄₁₆-in. by 5½-in.-long bolt, with two washers (one for the counter-bored hole on the post and one for the nut recess on the rail) and a nut. Tighten securely with a ½-in. nut driver. You may need to use a screwdriver to wedge the nut to keep it from turning as you tighten the bolt.

2. Slip the headboard tenon into its mortise on the attached post. Then slip the opposite post into place on both the headboard tenon and the alignment pins on the rail; then bolt together as in Step 1.

3. Next, assemble the footboard section in the same way.

4. Attach one end of one of the side rails to the headboard or footboard; then attach the other end of the same side rail.

5. Finally, insert the opposite side rail into place, bolt, and tighten.

6. Check to be sure all of the bolts are tight.

7. Drop the slat platform into place and secure it to the cleats with one screw in each corner.

Finishing

I finished the bed with an oil-and-wax finish. I applied the finish well ahead of when the piece would be needed, to ensure that any solvents would have evaporated fully.

PANEL BED

THIS IS A BED THAT CAN WORK a number of ways. Make it as a simple twin bed, with or without the footboard. Make two identical beds; rearrange the headboards and footboards so the two headboards are together on one bed, and the two footboards are together on the other; add metal pins to connect the footboard bed on top of the headboard bed; and you've got a set of bunk beds, needing only some guardrails and a ladder to complete the package. Or make the bed a different size altogether and wind up with a fun bed for an older (or a lot older) child. The design for this bed comes out of the work I did on the Toy Chest (p. 138), which I designed first. I liked the row of holes. Here, the holes go all the way through the upper rail on the bed and lighten up both the headboard and the footboard. If you're feeling more ambitious and are so inclined, try cutting squares or triangles.

PANEL BED

THE HEADBOARD AND FOOTBOARD are both assembled as complete units. The side rails bolt to the headboard and footboard to complete the bed frame (allowing for easy assembly and disassembly). The slats then drop into place. The dowel pins on the cleats keep the slats from sliding around.

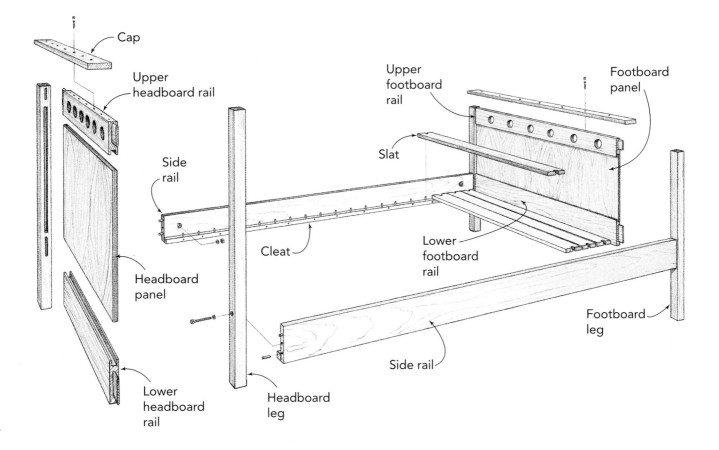

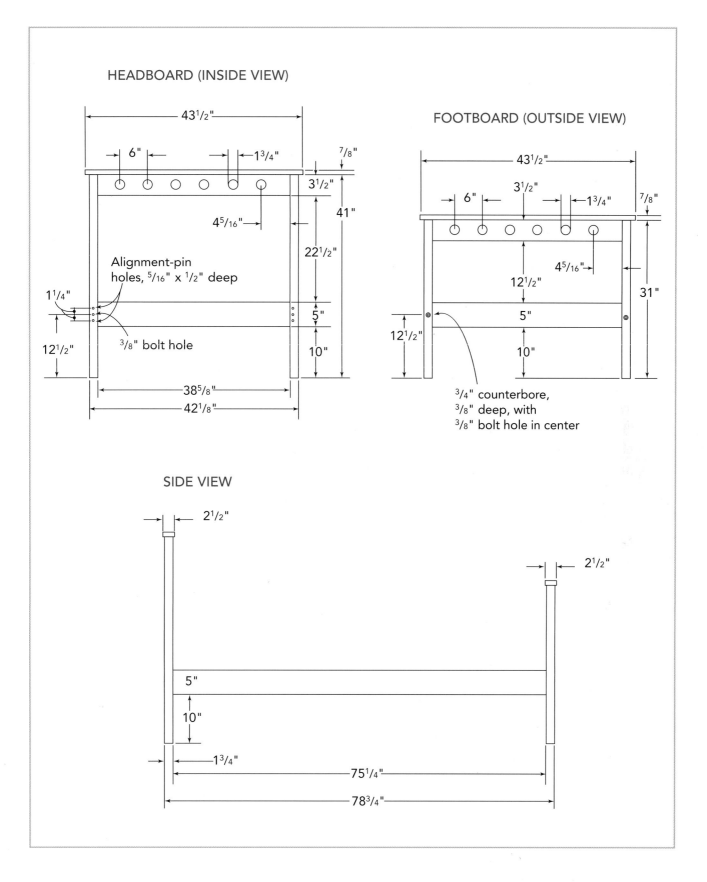

HEADBOARD (INSIDE VIEW)

43¹/₂"
6"
1³/₄"
⁷/₈"
3¹/₂"
41"
4⁵/₁₆"
22¹/₂"
Alignment-pin
holes, ⁵/₁₆" x ¹/₂" deep
1¹/₄"
5"
³/₈" bolt hole
12¹/₂"
10"
38⁵/₈"
42¹/₈"

FOOTBOARD (OUTSIDE VIEW)

43¹/₂"
6"
3¹/₂"
1³/₄"
⁷/₈"
4⁵/₁₆"
12¹/₂"
31"
12¹/₂"
5"
10"
³/₄" counterbore,
³/₈" deep, with
³/₈" bolt hole in center

SIDE VIEW

2¹/₂"
2¹/₂"
5"
10"
1³/₄"
75¹/₄"
78³/₄"

CUT LIST FOR PANEL BED		
2	Headboard legs	1¾" x 1¾" x 41¾"
2	Footboard legs	1¾" x 1¾" x 31¾"
1	Headboard panel	¾" plywood, 38$^{15}/_{16}$" x 23$^{7}/_{16}$"
1	Footboard panel	¾" plywood, 38$^{15}/_{16}$" x 13$^{7}/_{16}$"
2	Headboard and footboard lower rails	1⅛" x 5" x 41$^{7}/_{16}$"
2	Headboard and footboard upper rails	1⅛" x 3½" x 41$^{7}/_{16}$"
2	Caps	⅞" x 2½" x 43½"
2	Side rails	1⅛" x 5" x 75¼"
2	Cleats	1" x 1¼" x 75¼"
15	Slats	¾" x 4" x 39"
Hardware		
38	Dowel pins	$^{5}/_{16}$" x 1¼"
4	Hex-head bolts	$^{5}/_{16}$" x 5½" with nuts and 8 washers
	Screws	#8 x 1⅝"
	Wooden plugs	

MANY OF THE CONSTRUCTION methods for this bed are very similar to, if not exactly the same as, those for the Child's Four-Poster Bed (p. 48). I used the same basic method for attaching the rails to the headboard and footboard and a similar method for supporting the mattress. The major difference is that here the headboard and footboard are assembled as complete units, and the side rails attach to them to complete the bed frame. Because the construction of the headboard and footboard is identical, other than a few dimensions, it is best to work on them both at the same time.

Making the Legs

1. Mill the stock for the legs to 1¾ in. square and cut to rough length. The rough lengths should be about ¾ in. longer than the finished lengths. This extra length (called a horn) helps keep the legs from splitting above the mortises as you fit the upper-rail tenons.

2. Mark out locations for the counterbored holes for the bolt heads in the outsides of all four legs 12½ in. up from the bottom of the legs and centered on the leg. Drill the ¾-in.-diameter holes ⅜ in. deep.

3. Drill a ⅜-in. hole through the center of the counterbore, but go only about halfway into the leg. Now flip the leg over and carefully mark the location of the bolt hole on the inside. Drill until you meet the hole from the outside. This eliminates the problem of the drill bit wandering as you drill through the thick leg and keeps the hole centered on both sides of the leg.

4. The lower-rail mortises are all ½ in. by 3 in. by 1½ in. deep. Lay out the mortise locations carefully; they are not all the same (see "Mortise Details"). Be sure you wind up with a left and a right leg for both the headboard and the footboard.

5. The upper-rail mortises are ½ in. by 2 in. and should be just ¼ in. down from the actual tops of the legs. Remember that you left a ¾-in. horn there, however, so the mortises should be 1 in. down from the tops.

6. Cut all of the mortises. I used a plunge router fitted with a ½-in. straight bit and a fence.

Mortise Details

LEFT HEADBOARD LEG

RIGHT FOOTBOARD LEG

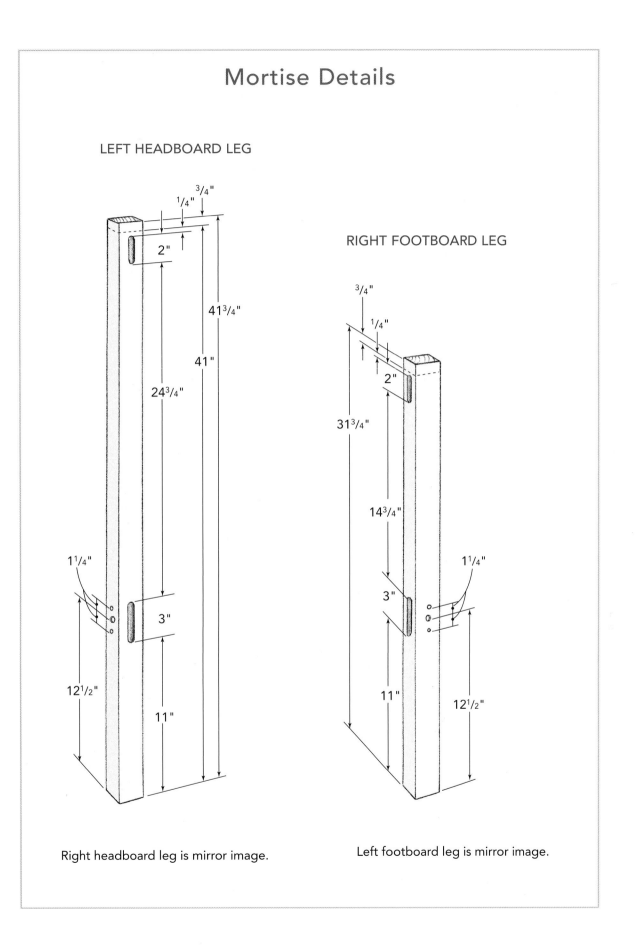

Right headboard leg is mirror image.

Left footboard leg is mirror image.

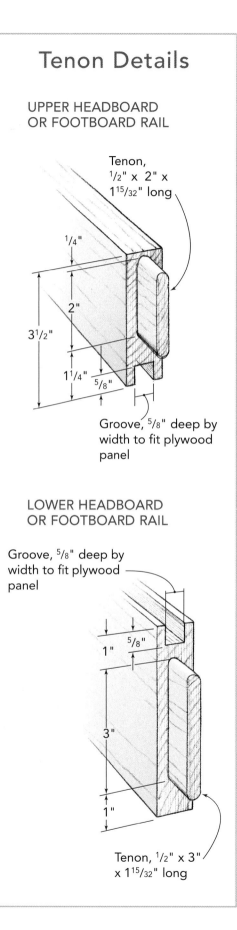

Tenon Details

UPPER HEADBOARD OR FOOTBOARD RAIL

Tenon, 1/2" x 2" x 1 15/32" long

1/4"

2"

3 1/2"

1 1/4"

5/8"

Groove, 5/8" deep by width to fit plywood panel

LOWER HEADBOARD OR FOOTBOARD RAIL

Groove, 5/8" deep by width to fit plywood panel

5/8"

1"

3"

1"

Tenon, 1/2" x 3" x 1 15/32" long

7. Use the alignment-pin drilling jig (p. 15) to drill the alignment-pin holes on the inside faces of the legs, opposite the counter-bored hole. These holes should be 1/2 in. deep. **8.** Plane or sand the legs. Be careful not to round over or change the angle of the faces that will join to the rails, or you will create gaps.

Making the Rails

1. Mill the stock for all of the rails at once. All are the same thickness.
2. Cut the side rails and lower headboard and footboard rails to 5 in. wide.
3. Cut the upper headboard and footboard rails to 3 1/2 in. wide.

Making the lower rails

The length of the rails (from tenon shoulder to tenon shoulder) determines the width of the bed. On this bed, the overall length of the rails must also include the length of the tenons. You can cut the rails to the lengths given in the cut list if all of your rails and posts are the specified thickness. If any of the dimensions are off, or if you are making a different size bed, you should calculate the exact lengths (see "Calculating Rail Lengths" on p. 58) and then add the tenon lengths based on your mortise depths.
1. Cut the lower headboard and footboard rails to length.
2. Cut the tenons on the ends of the rails (see "Tenon Details"). I cut the tenons on the table saw. Make sure that the length between the tenons is exactly what you need. I normally cut one tenon and then measure from the shoulder to mark out the location of the other shoulder. Slight variations in tenon length will not be important.
3. Round over the corners of the tenons with a rasp, so that they fit in the routed mortises. Fit the tenons carefully to the mortises. Mark what piece goes where.
4. Plane or sand the rails.
5. You need to cut the grooves for the panel, but this should wait until you have completed the upper headboard and footboard rails.

Making the upper rails

The length of the upper headboard and footboard rails needs to match that of the lower rails exactly (especially between the tenons).

1. Cut the tenon on one end of each of the upper rails. Be sure to lay out the tenon locations carefully. They are offset toward the top of the rails (see "Side-Rail Joinery Details").

2. Match up each upper rail with its lower counterpart. Place the lower rail on top of the upper and line up an edge and the shoulders of the tenoned ends exactly. Scribe the location of the opposite shoulder with a knife (see **Photo A**).

3. Now cut the opposite tenon.

4. Fit the tenons to the mortises in the legs and mark which tenon goes in which mortise.

5. Plane or sand the faces of the rails.

6. Lay out and drill the six 1¾-in. holes in each upper rail. Sand the insides of the holes smooth (a drum sander mounted in a drill press works well for this) and chamfer or round over the edges of the holes.

7. Now set up a dado head on the table saw and cut the ⅜-in.-deep grooves for the plywood panel on both the upper and the lower rails. Be sure you cut the grooves on the bottom edge of the upper rails (the edge farther away from the tenons). You can use the same setup to cut the grooves on the top edge of the lower rails. Test the fit of the plywood and adjust the groove if necessary.

Making the side rails

There is a little more leeway in the length of the side rails, so these can be simply cut to length.

1. Cut the rails to 75¼ in. long.

2. Drill the ⅜-in. hole for the bolt in the center of each end of the rails. Use a self-centering drill guide and drill as deep as possible. Then remove the guide and deepen the hole until it is at least 3½ in. deep.

3. Use the alignment-pin drilling jig (p. 15) to drill the holes for the ⁵⁄₁₆-in. alignment pins. These holes should be ⅞ in. deep (see "Side-Rail Joinery Details").

PHOTO A: Use the lower rail as your ruler for marking out the length of the upper rail between the shoulders. With the shoulders on one end perfectly flush, scribe the location of the opposite end of the upper rail from the lower rail shoulder.

Side-Rail Joinery Details

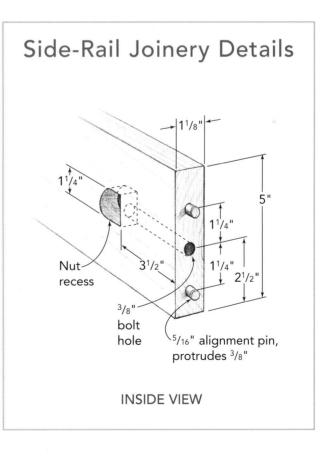

$1\frac{1}{8}$"

$1\frac{1}{4}$"

5"

$1\frac{1}{4}$"

Nut recess

$3\frac{1}{2}$"

$1\frac{1}{4}$"

$2\frac{1}{2}$"

$\frac{3}{8}$" bolt hole

$\frac{5}{16}$" alignment pin, protrudes $\frac{3}{8}$"

INSIDE VIEW

PHOTO B: Chisel the side of the nut recess closest to the end of the rail flat and square. Keep the chisel positioned across the grain; then finish up the sides of the hole with a couple of paring cuts along the grain.

4. Make the recess for the nut. Set up a drill press with a 1¼-in. Forstner bit and drill a ¹⁵⁄₁₆-in.-deep hole in the inside face of both ends of each rail. Check before drilling that the point of the Forstner bit will not come through to the outside face of the rail. The nut recess can also be routed if you prefer. In either case, try to leave at least ³⁄₁₆ in. of wood at the bottom of the hole, or this spot on the rail will be fragile.

5. Chisel a flat on the side of the hole closest to the ends (see **Photo B**).

6. Smooth the rails. Then chamfer all but the bottom inside edge, which is where the cleat will go.

Fitting the Panels in the Legs

You still need to cut grooves in the legs for the headboard and footboard panels. These grooves must match up exactly with the grooves in the rails.

1. Insert a rail tenon into its mortise and transfer the location of the groove to the leg with a sharp knife (see **Photo C**). Repeat this for each of the rail tenons, until all four legs are marked for the groove location on both the top and the bottom.

2. Set up a plunge router with a fence and a ½-in. straight bit (you'll cut the groove for the nominally ¾-in.-thick plywood panels in two passes). Clamp a leg to your workbench and set the matching leg next to it to help support the base of the router. Adjust the fence so that the router bit is close to, but not touching, one of the scribed layout lines for the groove. Slide the router to the other end of the groove to check that you won't rout over that line. Then rout the groove to ⅜ in. deep (see **Photo D**).

3. Check the distance between the groove and the layout lines at both the top and the bottom. If the groove seems to be in the right location, go ahead and adjust the fence and rout to the lines. Verify that the grooves

PHOTO C: Transfer the location of the panel groove from the rail onto the leg by marking with a knife.

PHOTO D: Using the second leg as a support for the router makes routing the groove for the panel safer and more accurate.

PHOTO E: The grooves in the legs and the rails must line up exactly. Selective sanding of the sides of the panel groove in the leg can help correct a minor misalignment.

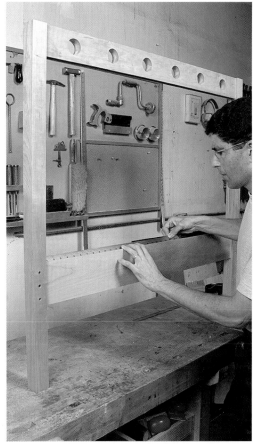

PHOTO F: Two rulers (or a stick of wood cut to a predetermined length and a ruler) make it easy to measure the length of the panel needed for the headboard or the footboard.

match up by reinserting the appropriate rail and test-fitting a piece of the plywood in the routed groove.

4. If the groove needs to be angled a little to match up with the grooves in the rails, you can use a simple trick to correct the problem (see "Routing Misaligned Panel Grooves" on p. 44). You can also try sanding the edges of the groove with sandpaper held on a thin block of wood (see **Photo E**).

5. Once the grooves all lined up and are the right size, dry-fit the headboard and footboard together and measure for the panel sizes (see **Photo F**). Leave a little bit of

room, especially in the height of the panel, to allow for the solid-wood rails to expand a little. Clearance of ⅛ in. from side to side is adequate, but you should leave ³⁄₁₆ in. clearance from top to bottom.

6. Cut the panels to size. Disassemble the headboard and footboard; then and reassemble them with the panels in place. Place the rails onto the panel before inserting the rails into the mortises in the legs.

7. While everything is together, scribe the tops of the legs flush with the upper rails, so you know where to cut them off. Then disassemble everything yet again.

Assembling the Headboard and Footboard

There are a few more things to do before the actual glue-up. Be sure to gather everything you'll need for gluing up the headboard and footboard before you start that process.

1. Cut the tops of the legs carefully to the scribed marks.

2. Smooth all of the parts and ease the edges. Chamfer the bottoms of the legs.

3. Glue-up is straightforward and should be relatively easy. Place the appropriate rails on the headboard or footboard panel. Spread glue in the mortises and then very lightly on the tenons; insert the tenons. Clamp up tightly.

4. When the glue is dry, remove the clamps and drill through the tenons that now block the ⅜-in. bolt holes in the legs.

Adding the Caps

The tops of the legs and the upper rail must be perfectly flush before you add the caps.

1. If the rails are a little high, you can plane them off carefully. Plane toward a leg, if possible, and stop before the plane iron goes off the leg to avoid chipping the leg.

2. If a leg is high, you can make up a very simple jig to rout it down perfectly flush with the rail (see "A Leg-Trimming Jig"). Make sure to rout clockwise around the outside of the leg in a shallow climb cut. This will prevent chipping of the edges of the leg (see **Photo G**).

3. Mill up the wood for the caps. Cut it to size and smooth the top surface and the edges. You can plane the bottom surface lightly, but don't sand it or you risk rounding it a little bit, which will make it difficult to fit tightly to the rail. Save some of the

PHOTO G: The leg-trimming jig makes it easy to rout the top of the leg perfectly flush with the upper rail.

PHOTO H: With just a little bit of glue on the top of the upper rail, position, clamp, and then screw the cap into place.

A Leg-Trimming Jig

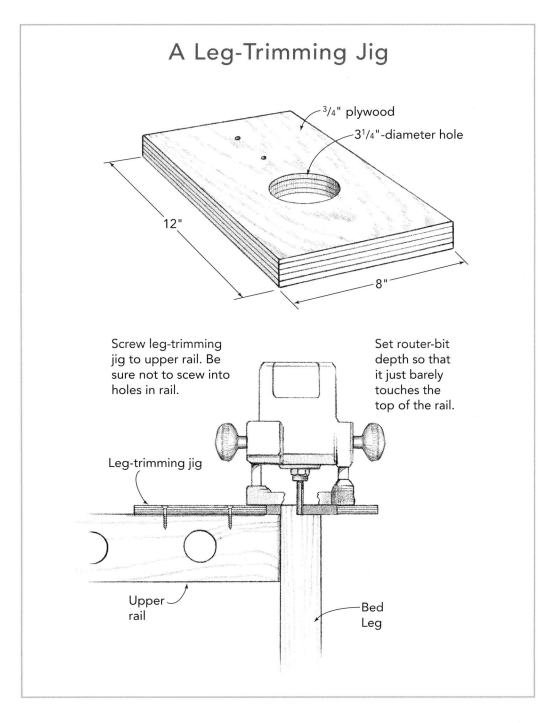

3/4" plywood

3 1/4"-diameter hole

12"

8"

Screw leg-trimming jig to upper rail. Be sure not to scew into holes in rail.

Set router-bit depth so that it just barely touches the top of the rail.

Leg-trimming jig

Upper rail

Bed Leg

scrap for making plugs to fill the counter-bores of the screw holes.

4. Drill counterbored pilot holes for the screws that will attach the caps to the rails.

5. Spread glue lightly on the top of the rail, set the cap down in place, adjust if necessary, and clamp to hold it while you screw it down (see **Photo H**). Drive all of the screws; then plug the holes.

6. Cut off the protruding plugs and then plane or sand smooth.

Finishing

The bed is essentially done. You should start on the finishing process now, and between coats you can work on the mattress support.

Cleat Detail

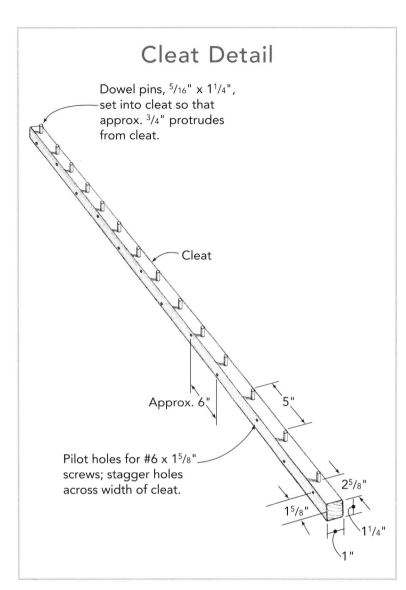

Dowel pins, $5/16$" x $1^1/4$", set into cleat so that approx. $3/4$" protrudes from cleat.

Cleat

Approx. 6"

5"

Pilot holes for #6 x $1^5/8$" screws; stagger holes across width of cleat.

$2^5/8$"

$1^5/8$"

$1^1/4$"

1"

PHOTO I: Start at one end of the cleat, clamp it into place, and tighten down the first screw. Then work your way across, making sure the cleat remains flush with the bottom of the rail as you go.

Making the Mattress Support

The mattress support consists of the cleats, which screw to the side rails, and the platform itself, which is made up of either slats or a piece of ¾-in. plywood.

Making the cleats

The cleats are strips of wood 1 in. by 1¼ in. by the length of the rails (see "Cleat Detail").
1. If you're making a slatted platform, drill holes for ⁵⁄₁₆-in. dowels (to locate the slats) in the upper edge of the strip. These holes should be spaced 5 in. apart and roughly centered on the edge.
2. Drill pilot holes for the screws that will attach the cleats to the rails. The holes should be in the wider face of the strip, about every 6 in. I usually stagger the holes across the width of the cleat. Shift holes if necessary to avoid drilling through a dowel hole.
3. Squirt a little glue into each dowel hole; then pound in a ⁵⁄₁₆-in. by 1¼-in. dowel.
4. Attach the cleats after the finish has been applied to the side rails. The cleats don't really need to be finished (see **Photo I**).

Making the slats

1. Mill up 15 slats out of a reasonably priced wood (soft maple and poplar are two of my usual choices; for wider beds, I use hard maple). The slats should be ¾ in. by 4 in. by the width of the bed inside the rails, less ½₂ in. to ¹⁄₁₆ in. (see "Slat Detail").

2. Cut a ⅜-in.-wide by ¾-in.-deep notch in the end of each slat. The notches can then slip over the dowel pins in the cleats, which keeps the slats from shifting around (see **Photo J**).

3. As an alternative to the slats, you can cut a piece of ¾-in. plywood to the size of the bed between the rails and between the headboard and footboard. You'll have to notch the corners for the legs.

Putting It All Together

Assembly is very similar to that of the Child's Four-Poster Bed (p. 48). Use ⁵⁄₁₆-in. by 5½-in. hex-head bolts with nuts and washers.

1. Place the guide pins on the end of a side rail into the corresponding holes in a leg of the headboard. Slip a bolt with a washer into the bolt hole, and thread this onto a washer and nut in the nut recess of the rail.

2. Tighten the bolt with a ½-in. nut driver while preventing the nut from turning on the inside of the rail by wedging either a ½-in. open-end wrench or a screwdriver against the nut.

3. Now attach the footboard to the opposite end of the side rail the same way.

4. Finally, raise the other rail into place, insert the guide pins of the other side rail into the holes in the legs, and bolt together. Go around the bed frame and check all of the bolts to make sure they are snug.

5. Lay the slats or plywood mattress platform in place, and the bed is finished.

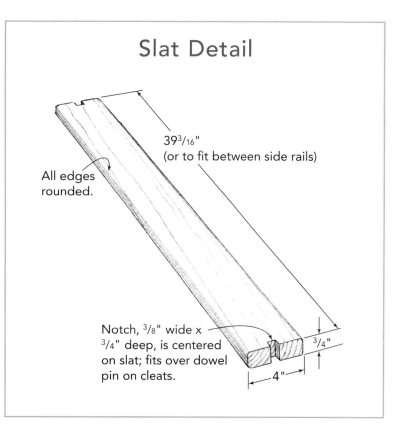

Slat Detail

All edges rounded.

39³⁄₁₆" (or to fit between side rails)

Notch, ³⁄₈" wide x ³⁄₄" deep, is centered on slat; fits over dowel pin on cleats.

³⁄₄"

4"

PHOTO J: The slots in the ends of the slats can be cut easily on the table saw, using a tenoning jig with a wooden fence attached to support the slat.

MAKING A BUNK BED

Two of these beds can be combined to make bunk beds by using 4-in.-long metal pins to connect the upper and lower beds and then making guardrails and a ladder for the top bunk.

Front and back guardrails are important for making the top bunk as safe as possible. The guardrails must extend up from the top of the mattress by at least 5 in. and should be attached securely to legs. Use metal pins embedded into the upper ends of guardrails that fit into holes in the legs. Tightening the side rail into place during assembly will lock the guardrail in position. Alternatively, you can use bolts and barrel nuts or threaded inserts.

You must secure the platform on the upper bunk by screwing it (slats or plywood) to the cleat. That way, a child kicking up from the bottom bunk can't dislodge the upper mattress platform. Finally, the ladder must be attached firmly to the bed rail so the child can safely climb into and out of the top bunk.

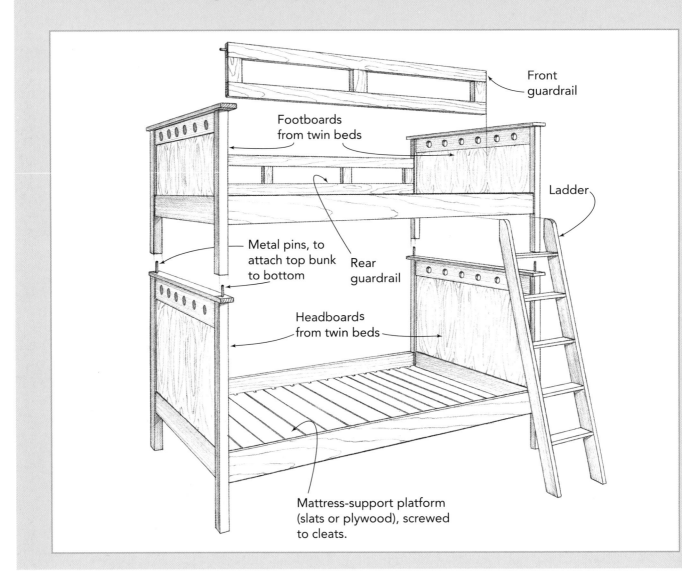

Front guardrail

Footboards from twin beds

Ladder

Metal pins, to attach top bunk to bottom

Rear guardrail

Headboards from twin beds

Mattress-support platform (slats or plywood), screwed to cleats.

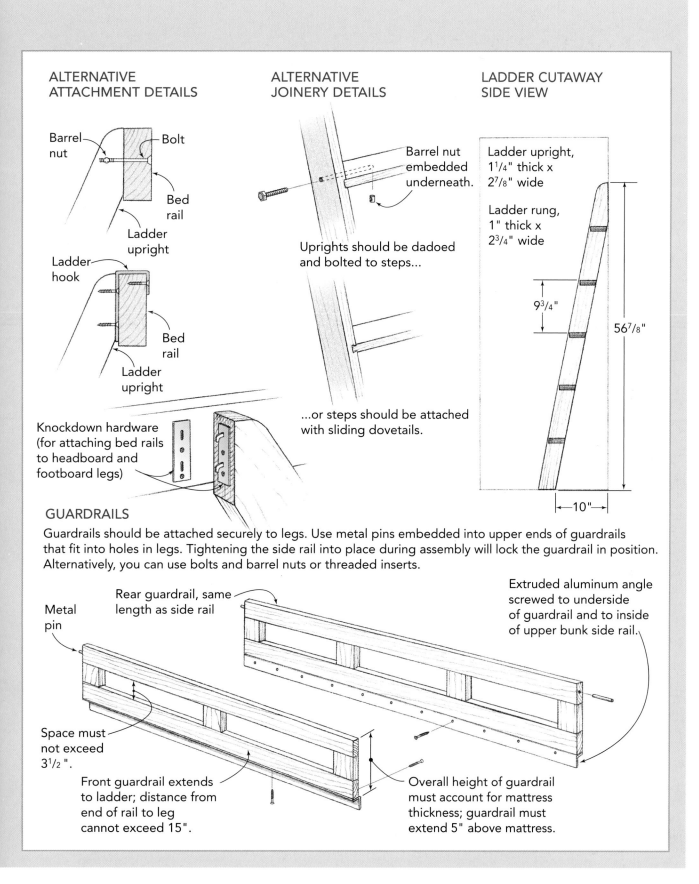

ALTERNATIVE ATTACHMENT DETAILS

Barrel nut

Bolt

Bed rail

Ladder upright

Ladder hook

Bed rail

Ladder upright

Knockdown hardware (for attaching bed rails to headboard and footboard legs)

ALTERNATIVE JOINERY DETAILS

Barrel nut embedded underneath.

Uprights should be dadoed and bolted to steps...

...or steps should be attached with sliding dovetails.

LADDER CUTAWAY SIDE VIEW

Ladder upright, 1¹⁄₄" thick x 2⁷⁄₈" wide

Ladder rung, 1" thick x 2³⁄₄" wide

9³⁄₄"

56⁷⁄₈"

10"

GUARDRAILS

Guardrails should be attached securely to legs. Use metal pins embedded into upper ends of guardrails that fit into holes in legs. Tightening the side rail into place during assembly will lock the guardrail in position. Alternatively, you can use bolts and barrel nuts or threaded inserts.

Rear guardrail, same length as side rail

Metal pin

Extruded aluminum angle screwed to underside of guardrail and to inside of upper bunk side rail.

Space must not exceed 3¹⁄₂".

Front guardrail extends to ladder; distance from end of rail to leg cannot exceed 15".

Overall height of guardrail must account for mattress thickness; guardrail must extend 5" above mattress.

A VERSATILE CHILDREN'S TABLE

HIS IS INDEED A VERSATILE PLAY TABLE. It's simple, sturdy, and the right height for use with a child's chair with a seat height of 10 in. to 11 in.—for use with the Marble Chair (p. 106), you may want to make these table legs a little taller. But the table can mature with your children. Start with a piece of melamine (or plastic laminate–covered) board edged with wood for use as a messy general-purpose table. As the child gets older (or for an older child to begin with), make a game table with a removable center panel. You can use it for one or more games or even as a chalkboard.

And once the kids are gone (or just out of the room), the table can work in a family room as a coffee table for the adults. A variety of grown-up things can go in the center, too. You can insert a piece of slate cut to the right size (the kids might like that if you left some chalk around). Or you can fit the table with a piece of glass—add a box under the glass, and you have a place to display objects or artwork from the kids or adults. The table itself is simple to construct. That leaves you room to make it into whatever you want.

A VERSATILE CHILDREN'S TABLE

THIS VERSATILE TABLE can incorporate a center panel that can be anything you choose, as straightforward or as challenging as you want. Here, the table has a checkerboard that's finished on the back with chalkboard paint. A simpler, alternate top is illustrated below.

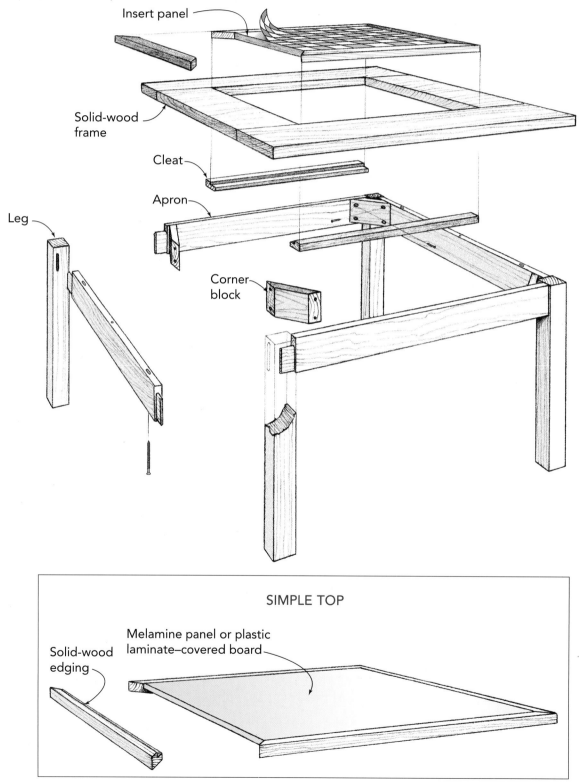

Insert panel

Solid-wood frame

Cleat

Apron

Leg

Corner block

SIMPLE TOP

Melamine panel or plastic laminate–covered board

Solid-wood edging

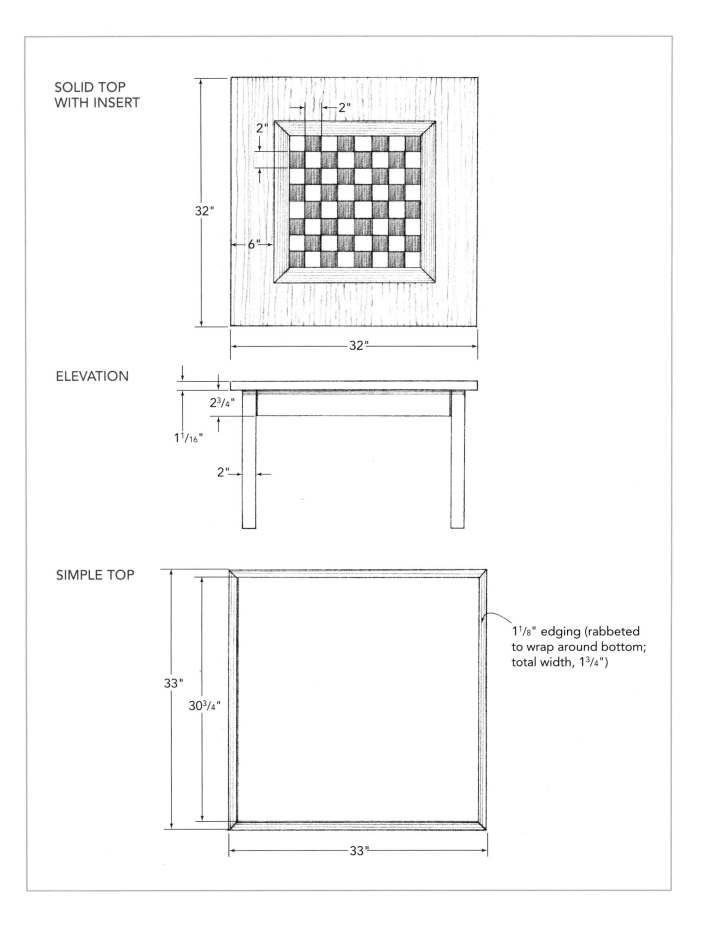

SOLID TOP
WITH INSERT

2"

2"

32"

6"

32"

ELEVATION

2³/₄"

1¹/₁₆"

2"

SIMPLE TOP

1¹/₈" edging (rabbeted
to wrap around bottom;
total width, 1³/₄")

33"

30³/₄"

33"

CUT LIST FOR A VERSATILE CHILDREN'S TABLE

4	Legs	2" x 2" x 16⅞"
4	Aprons	¾" (at least) x 2¾" x 27¼"
4	Corner blocks	1¼" x 2½" x 5"
With the Simple Top		
1	Melamine panel	⅝" x 30¾" x 30¾"
4	Pieces of edging	1⁄16" x 1¾" x 33"
With the Insert-Panel Top		
1	Solid-wood top	1⁄16" x 32" x 32"*
2	Cleats	¾" x 2½" x 20⅛"
1	Substrate (MDF or plywood)	¾" x 24" x 24"
4	Solid-wood edging stock for the checkerboard	⅞" x 2" x 24"
	Veneer game board or material for homemade game board	
Hardware		
4	Glides for leg bottoms	
6	Screws	#8 x 3"
16	Screws	#6 x 1¼"

*With 20⅛" x 20⅛" opening in center.

THIS PROJECT naturally falls into two phases: the base and the top. The top can be broken down further into the frame and the insert components. Each phase is an easily manageable project, and each has its own challenges, from the joinery of the base to the laying up of a checkerboard for the insert.

Making the Base

The base for the table is a good place to start, because it is simple and straightforward. I suggest using mortise-and-tenon joinery backed up with corner blocks, but you can opt for simpler methods if you choose. A pair of dowels for each joint will work if you use the corner blocks to reinforce them, as will metal leg brackets.

Making the legs

1. Mill up the stock for the legs to 2 in. square and cut all four to 16⅞ in. long.
2. Lay out the ⅜-in. by 2-in. mortises in the legs as shown in "Mortise-and-Tenon Layout." Note that the two mortises on each leg are symmetrical but require two different setups if you will be cutting them by machine.
3. I used a plunge router in conjunction with a very simple jig I call a mortising block to cut the mortises (see "Mortising Block" on p. 12). This makes the mortising quick, accurate, and easily repeatable (see **Photo A**).

Making the aprons

I made the apron out of 6/4 stock, because I had some around, but the exact thickness is not critical; 4/4 and 5/4 wood will work as

PHOTO A: Routing the mortises in the legs is easy with a plunge router. Make several shallow passes with the router, not a single full-depth pass, to get the best results.

well. Just be sure you lay out the tenons by referencing off the outside face of the apron.

1. The apron stock should be at least ¾ in. thick but can be thicker. Mill the stock to 27¼ in. to include the tenons, although ultimately the length between the shoulders will be 25 in.

2. Begin laying out for the tenons by scribing the shoulders on one of the pieces. A marking gauge with a sharp knife (or a point filed so it cuts like a knife) is the best tool for the job.

3. The tenon should be ³⁄₁₆ in. from the outside face of the apron.

4. I cut these tenons on the table saw, simply laying the pieces flat on the saw table and cutting away the waste (see "Tenons Flat on the Table Saw" on p. 13). Adjust the height of the blade to cut just up to the marked-out line for the tenon cheek. I used the rip fence with a block clamped on to it

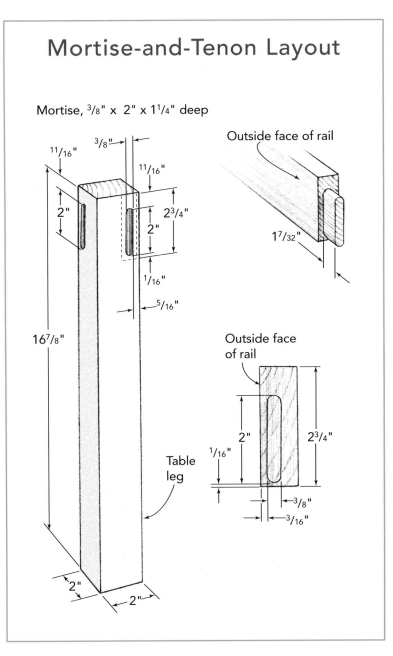

Mortise-and-Tenon Layout

Mortise, ³⁄₈" x 2" x 1¼" deep

Outside face of rail

Table leg

Outside face of rail

TIP

It is helpful to treat each piece of wood you work with as if it had its position marked out all over it. You should keep in mind throughout the project how every part will be oriented in the final piece. You may want to mark what goes where and how it should go there—especially for pieces that are not readily obvious.

PHOTO B: Fitting tenons is what a rabbet plane does best. Hold the plane flat and cut across the grain.

PHOTO C: Gluing up in two stages is a much calmer process than doing it all at once. Start with gluing the legs to two (opposite!) aprons. Filler blocks keep the apron mortises from being crushed.

> **TIP**
>
> Make sure to spread as little glue as possible on the tenons. Any excess will just squeeze out of the joint as it goes together, making for more work later.

as a stop to locate the shoulders for the tenon in the right place. You may have to readjust the blade height when you cut the inside face of the tenon and when you cut the top and bottom.

5. Fit the tenons to the mortises one at a time, using a plane (sometimes called a cheek plane or a shoulder plane), a rasp, or a piece of sandpaper on a block of wood (see **Photo B**). However you remove the wood, proceed carefully so you wind up with a snug fit. You should be able to put the joint together by hand, but it should feel

tight. If you wind up with a loose fit, you can glue on a thin shim of wood and then refit the joint.

6. Mark the mating mortise and tenon with a matching letter or number as you fit them.

Preparing the base parts for glue-up

1. Plane, scrape, or sand the legs and the aprons. Be careful not to round over the areas around the mortises on the legs. You don't have to smooth the top edge of the aprons, and the inside face is entirely optional.

2. Chamfer the four edges of the legs and the bottom two edges of the aprons. You can sand, plane, or rout these small chamfers.

3. Also chamfer the bottom edges of each of the legs. This helps keep the bottoms of the legs from chipping off when the table is moved around.

Gluing up the base

It is much easier to glue up the base in two stages, attaching the legs to the opposite aprons to start.

1. Prepare for gluing up the base by gathering clamps, clamp pads, glue, and scraps of wood to spread the glue in the mortises and on the tenons. You'll also need four small scraps of wood (about 1 in. by 1½ in.) milled to fit in the mortises. These filler blocks will protect the walls of the mortises from being crushed by the clamps.

2. Spread glue in the mortises and very lightly on the tenons; then insert the appropriate tenon into its mortise and push together as far as you can. Repeat on the other side.

3. Insert the filler blocks into the open mortises and clamp the legs to the apron (see **Photo C**).

4. Repeat with the other legs and apron. Let the glue dry before proceeding to the final assembly of the base.

5. Remove the clamps and the filler blocks; then spread glue in the remaining mortises and sparingly on the tenons, insert the apron tenons into the legs on one side and then on the other (see **Photo D**).

6. Clamp up the base.

PHOTO D: Fit the aprons to one sub-assembly, carefully work the opposite subassembly into place, and then add clamps.

PHOTO E: There's enough room inside the aprons to use a cordless drill to drive the screws into the corner blocks.

Making the corner blocks

The corner blocks do not have to be made from the same material as the rest of the table, although they certainly can be.

1. Mill the stock for the corner blocks (see "Making the Corner Blocks").

2. Set the blade on the table saw to 45 degrees and cut the corner blocks to 5 in. long. It is safest to clamp the corner block stock to the miter guide of the table saw for each cut.

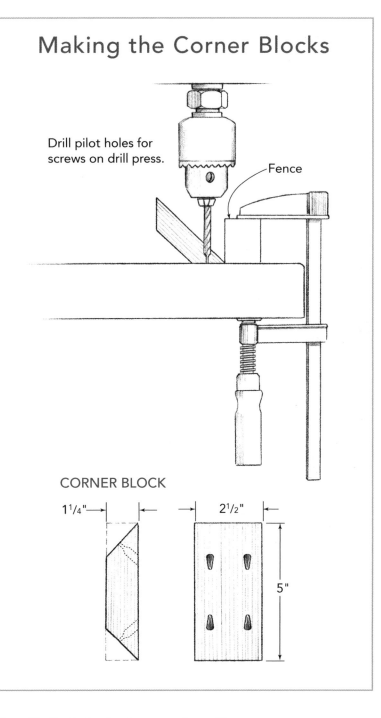

Making the Corner Blocks

Drill pilot holes for screws on drill press.

Fence

CORNER BLOCK

1¹/₄"

2¹/₂"

5"

3. Drill pilot holes for the screws that will attach the corner blocks to the aprons. There should be two screws on each side of every corner block.

4. It is much easier to attach the corner blocks to the table base after you apply the finish to the table. That way, you avoid having to finish around the awkward blocks (see **Photo E**).

Making the Tabletops

Making the simple top

1. Start with a piece of ⅝-in.-thick melamine-coated board cut to 30¾ in. square or face a piece of plywood or particleboard with plastic laminate.

2. Make up the rabbeted solid-wood edging to fit around the center panel (see "The Simple Top").

3. Miter the ends of the edging to fit.

4. Glue and screw the edging in place.

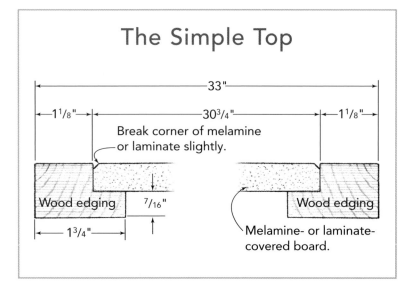

The Simple Top

33"

1⅛" — 30¾" — 1⅛"

Break corner of melamine or laminate slightly.

Wood edging   7/16"   Wood edging

1¾"

Melamine- or laminate-covered board.

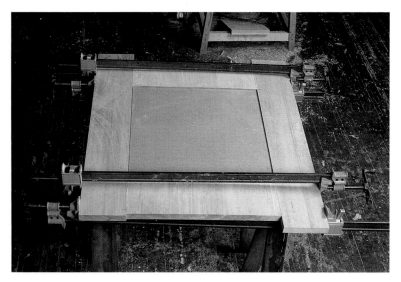

PHOTO F: Using a spacer panel the size of the insert is a critical part of getting the opening of this tabletop just right.

Making the insert-panel top

The insert panel It makes sense to start with the insert panel, since it is relatively easy to size the overall top to fit around it. I made a checkerboard for the insert panel (see "Making a Checkerboard" on p. 88). If you're looking for an easy way to do this, simply purchase a veneer checkerboard ready to be adhered to a substrate panel (see "Sources" on p. 151).

Bear in mind that you have to balance what you do on one side of the panel with something similar on the other side. I veneered the opposite side of the insert and then painted it with chalkboard paint from my local paint store. You can also purchase a backgammon board that is ready to be glued onto the panel.

The insert frame The insert sits in a solid-wood frame. It is built with the grain all running in the same direction. It is easy to do this if you glue up the short-grain sections first.

1. Start by gluing up a 1¹⁄₁₆-in.-thick wood panel that is roughly 14 in. long by 21 in. wide.

2. Sand or plane the panel smooth. Then cut it into two pieces that are about 6½ in. long and exactly 20⅛ in. wide.

3. Sand one of the end-grain edges of each piece. These will be the inside of the opening for the insert and will be much more difficult to sand later.

4. Prepare two 1¹⁄₁₆-in.-thick pieces of wood that are 6 in. wide and 33 in. long.

5. Cut a piece of scrap ¾-in. plywood 20 in. by 20⅛ in. (or ⅛ in. larger than the insert if it is not exactly 20 in.) to use as a spacer when gluing up the top. This spacer will keep the two short-grain pieces of the top the proper distance apart, but you need a little clearance in the other direction to ensure the pieces can be clamped together.

6. Glue the two 6-in.-wide pieces to the two 20⅛-in.-wide pieces, using the plywood spacer board to keep the short-grain pieces 20⅛ in. apart (see **Photo F** and "A Reversible-Insert Top").

PHOTO G: It is very easy to sand a frame like this out of level. Use a large sanding block—with the sandpaper glued to the bottom.

7. When the glue is dry, trim the top to 32 in. by 32 in., then sand the top and bottom smooth and flush (see **Photo G**).

The cleats Make up two cleats to support the insert in the frame's opening. Because the insert panel is likely to be thinner than the frame, the cleats should be L-shaped pieces that screw to the underside of the frame and extend up into the opening.
1. Measure the thickness of the frame and that of the insert. The difference between the two is how much the cleat needs to extend up into the opening.
2. Mill the cleats to the dimensions given in the cut list. Rabbet the cleats, leaving a portion of the stock protruding that is ¾ in. wide and as thick as the difference between the top and insert thicknesses (see "Adding the Cleats"). When the insert rests on the rabbet, the top of the insert should be flush with the top of the solid-wood frame.
3. Drill the molding strips with countersunk holes for screws and attach the cleats to the two long-grain edges of the underside of the frame.

A Reversible-Insert Top

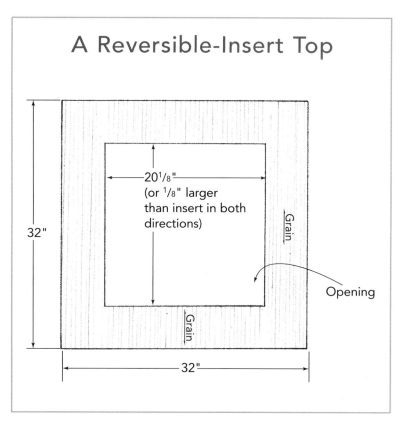

32"

$20^1/_8$"
(or $^1/_8$" larger than insert in both directions)

Grain

Grain

Opening

32"

Adding the Cleats

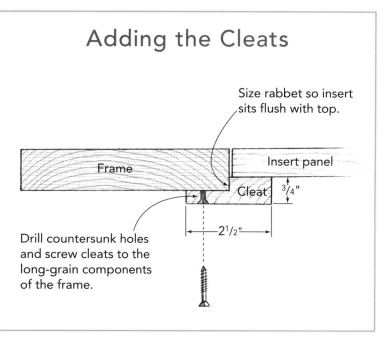

Size rabbet so insert sits flush with top.

Frame

Insert panel

Cleat

¾"

Drill countersunk holes and screw cleats to the long-grain components of the frame.

$2^1/_2$"

MAKING A CHECKERBOARD

1. Mill up ½-in.- to ¾-in.-thick by 2-in.-wide by 42-in.-long strips of two contrasting woods. You'll need at least four strips of each wood.

2. Glue four strips together, alternating dark, light, dark, light. Let the glue dry.

3. Plane the striped boards smooth; then mill to ⅛ in. thick.

4. Crosscut the striped boards into 2-in.-wide lengths. This step is the critical one; the cuts must be square and exactly the same width.

5. Tape the pieces together into a checkerboard pattern, using clear plastic packaging tape or masking tape. You can stretch either of these tapes a little as you're applying them to hold the pieces together tightly.

6. Glue the taped-up checkerboard down to an oversize substrate of medium-density fiberboard (MDF) or plywood.

7. To ensure that the panel will be stable, veneer the opposite side of the substrate with wood of equal thickness.

8. Trim the board to size; then edge it with 2-in.-wide strips of solid wood the same thickness as the veneered panel. You might sandwich a couple of pieces of veneer as a decorative accent between the panel and the edging. Miter the corners of all pieces carefully. Glue on two opposite sides first and then the remaining two.

9. Sand smooth.

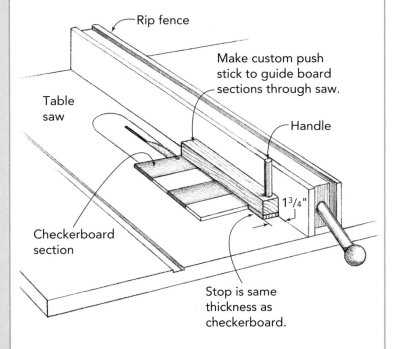

You can make your own checkerboard out of solid stock or buy a premade veneer checkerboard ready to glue down to the substrate.

Attaching the Tabletop

1. In the bottom edge of two opposite aprons, drill countersunk holes about ¼ in. deep for the six screws that will attach the top to the base. For each apron, drill one hole in the middle and one at each end (see "Attaching the Top").

2. Flip the base right side up, and drill down from the top 1½ in. into the four outer holes with a ⅜-in. drill bit. This will leave room for the tabletop to expand and contract with changes in humidity.

3. Place the top upside down on a padded surface and place the table base, also upside down, on it. Be sure that the grain of the top runs perpendicular to the aprons with the screw holes in them.

4. Center the base carefully on the top (see **Photo H**).

5. Check to be sure you have the correct screw size: #8 x 3 in., but be sure you won't screw through the top. Then drive the screws in to secure the base to the top.

Finishing

1. Apply your finish of choice.

2. Hammer the glides onto the bottoms of the legs to protect both the floor and the legs.

3. Challenge a young friend to a game.

4. Lose gracefully.

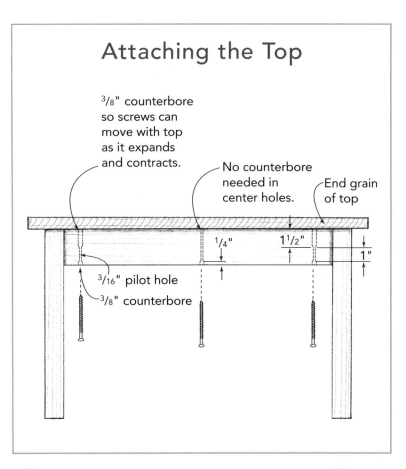

Attaching the Top

⅜" counterbore so screws can move with top as it expands and contracts.

No counterbore needed in center holes.

End grain of top

¼"

1½"

1"

³⁄₁₆" pilot hole

⅜" counterbore

PHOTO H: Take time to get the base centered on the top. Measure from both faces of all four legs. When the base is properly positioned, hold it tightly in place and drive in the screws.

CHILD'S ROCKER

KIDS ARE ALWAYS IN MOTION. It's not easy to get them even to sit down in a chair. But this rocker lets them work off energy while staying in one place. And rocking can be just as soothing for children as it tends to be for adults. Kids love it.

The construction is a combination of the typical and the unusual; although there are simple dadoes routed in the plywood panels to align the parts, everything is held together with ¼-in. threaded rods and cap nuts. This makes it sturdy enough to withstand the typical amount of abuse that kids will dish out but also easy to knock down and store (or ship) flat.

There are lots of ways to finish this rocker to get different results. I've gone with interesting colors as well as a basic oil-and-wax finish. But that doesn't mean you can't come up with your own design scheme, or just let the child decorate it the way he or she wishes.

CHILD'S ROCKER

THE ROCKER IS MADE OF FIVE SHAPED pieces of plywood. Shallow dadoes in the plywood sides and back locate the parts in the proper positions, and the whole thing is held together with two threaded rods tensioned with cap nuts.

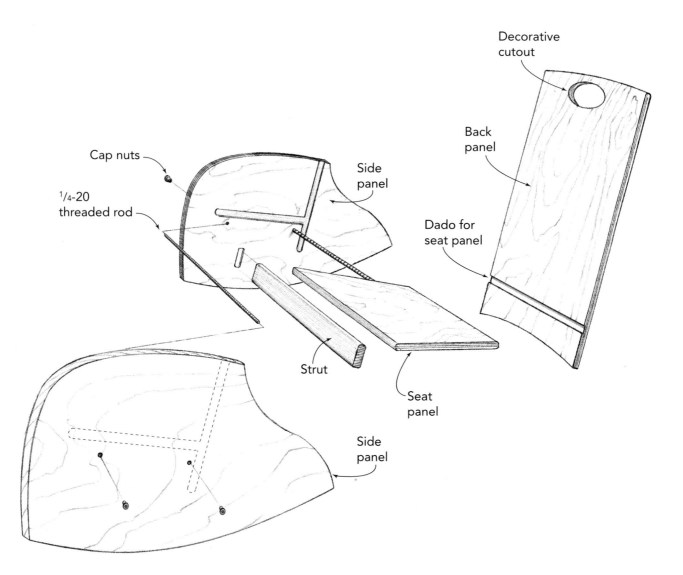

Decorative cutout

Back panel

Cap nuts

Side panel

1/4-20 threaded rod

Dado for seat panel

Strut

Seat panel

Side panel

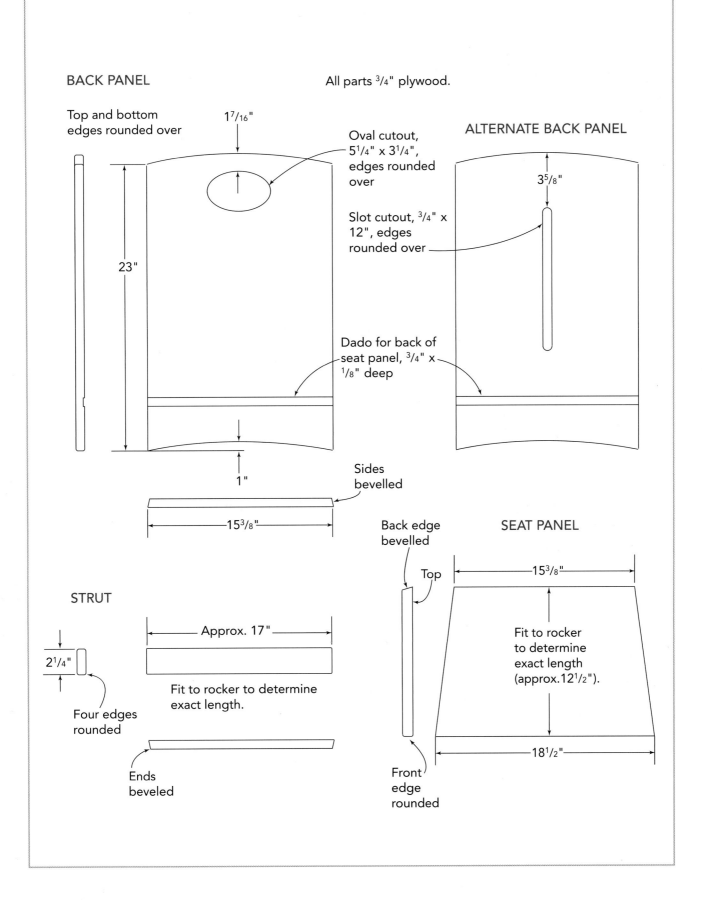

BACK PANEL

All parts ³/₄" plywood.

Top and bottom edges rounded over

1⁷/₁₆"

Oval cutout, 5¹/₄" x 3¹/₄", edges rounded over

ALTERNATE BACK PANEL

3⁵/₈"

Slot cutout, ³/₄" x 12", edges rounded over

23"

Dado for back of seat panel, ³/₄" x ¹/₈" deep

1"

Sides bevelled

15³/₈"

STRUT

2¹/₄"

Approx. 17"

Fit to rocker to determine exact length.

Four edges rounded

Ends beveled

Back edge bevelled

SEAT PANEL

Top

15³/₈"

Fit to rocker to determine exact length (approx.12¹/₂").

18¹/₂"

Front edge rounded

CUT LIST FOR CHILD'S ROCKER

2	Side panels	¾" x 16" x 26"*
1	Seat panel	¾" x 12½" x 18½"
1	Back panel	¾" x 15⅜" x 24⅛"
1	Strut	¾" x 2¼" x 17"
Hardware		
1	Threaded rod	¼-20 x 36" long**
4	Cap nuts	¼-20***
Miscellaneous		
	Scrap wood for interim jig	½"–¾" x 8" x 18"
	Plywood for side panel jig	¾" x 25" x 32"

*All parts are Baltic birch plywood or equivalent.
**Cut into two pieces based on measurements from completed chair.
***Also called connector nuts; typically used with connector bolts.

THE FIRST STEP in making the rocker is to make up a jig for locating the dadoes for the seat, the back, and the strut on the side panels. Because the relationship of the seat parts to the curve of the rocker is so important, you'll also use the side panel jig to define the shape and location of the rocker relative to the dadoes and thus to the seat and back of the rocker.

Making the Side-Panel Jig

Make the jig for the side panels out of a piece of ¾-in. by 25-in. by 32-in. plywood (see "Side-Panel Dado Jig").

1. Draw a reference line 15 in. from (and parallel to) one of the long edges of the plywood. I measured from the left edge, and that's what is shown here. You will reference off of this edge when routing the actual side panels. Mark it now as your reference edge.

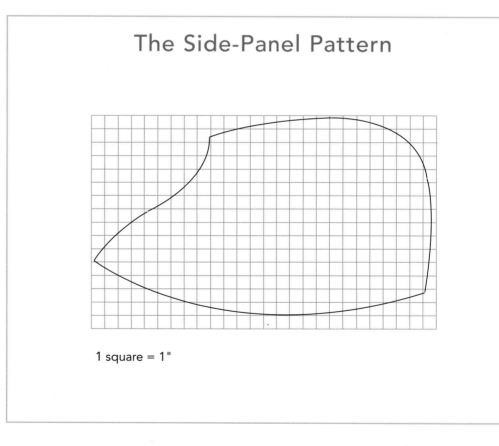

The Side-Panel Pattern

1 square = 1"

Side-Panel Dado Jig

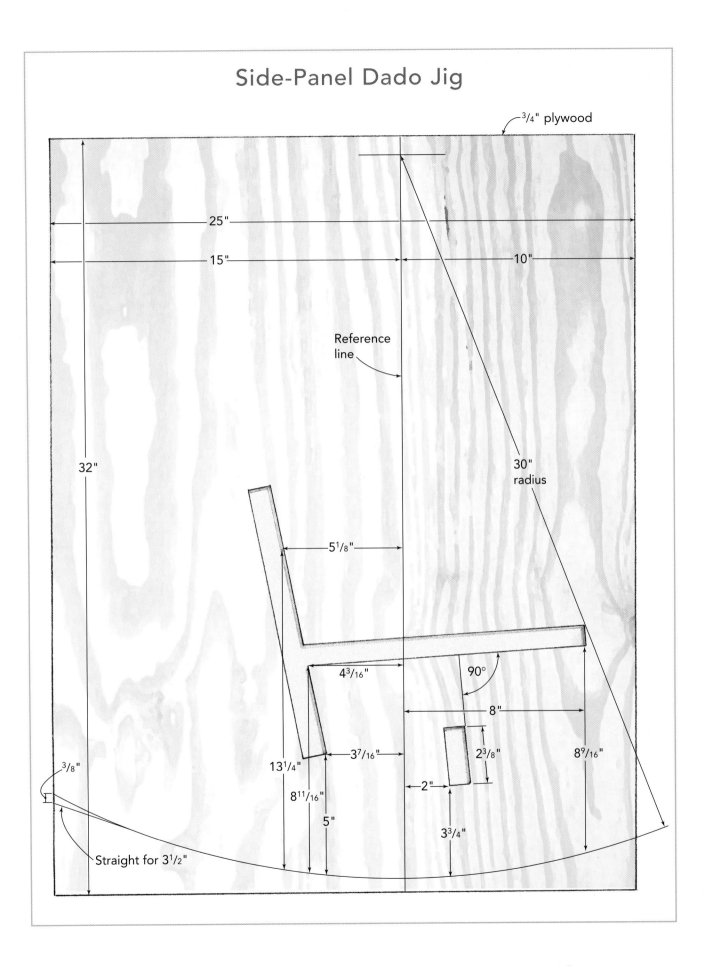

3/4" plywood

25"

15"

10"

Reference line

32"

30" radius

5 1/8"

4 3/16"

90°

8"

13 1/4"

3 7/16"

2 3/8"

8 9/16"

8 11/16"

2"

5"

3 3/4"

3/8"

Straight for 3 1/2"

MAKING THE INTERIM SLOT JIG

The interim jig is built up to have a ⅞-in.-wide by 12½-in.-long slot down the middle of it. The jig is then used with a flush-trimming bit to cut the slots in the side panel jig.

1. Cut apart a board roughly 18 in. long by 8 in. wide by ½ in. to ¾ in. thick into two 3⁷⁄₁₆-in.-wide strips and one strip exactly ⅞ in. wide.

2. Crosscut the ⅞-in.- wide strip into three parts; one 12½ in. long, and two about 2⅝ in. long. Set aside the 12½-in.-long strip; it will be used later when routing the short slot for the strut.

3. Glue the two 2⅝-in. pieces in between the two 3⁷⁄₁₆-in.- wide strips, with the ends of both short and long pieces flush. This should leave a ⅞-in. by 12½-in. slot in the middle.

4. Plane the faces of the jig smooth once the glue has dried.

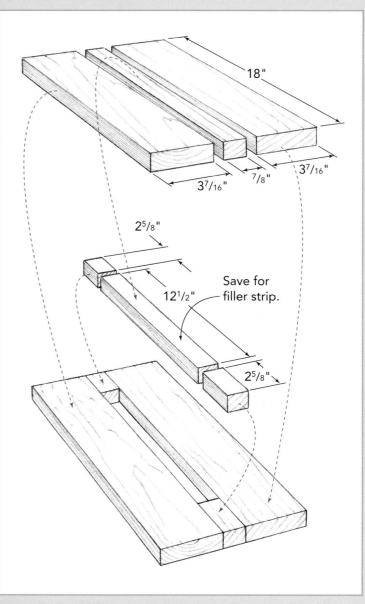

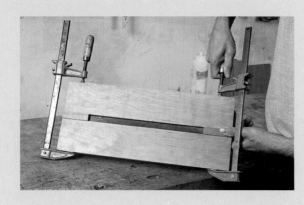

Making a jig to make another jig may seem like a lot of trouble, but the interim jig helps get the slots in the side panel jig located and sized correctly.

2. Next, mark out the curve of the rocker. The rocker is mostly an arc of a circle with a 30-in. radius. Mark the center point of the arc on the reference line, about 1 in. down from the top of the plywood. Using a scrap of ¼-in. plywood or a long thin scrap of wood, make up a "compass" by drilling one hole for a nail and another hole, 30 in. away, for a pencil point. Scribe the arc across the bottom of the plywood.

3. The back of the rocker will end about ⅛ in. away from the left edge of the plywood after it gets rounded over. The front of the rocker extends all the way to the other side of the plywood.

4. Flatten out the back 3½ in. of the rocker to make it harder to tip the chair over. Measure down ¾ in. from the arc along the back edge of the jig, then draw a 3½-in.-long straight line from this point to the arc of the rocker.

5. Now you're ready to locate the dadoes for the seat, back, and strut. Measure over from the reference line and up from the arc of the rocker to locate the various points shown in "Side-Panel Dado Jig" on p. 95 that will define the locations the dadoes. Make sure all of the lines are perpendicular or parallel to the reference line.

6. The dadoes themselves will be ¾ in. wide, but because you are making a jig that will be used with a ⅝-in. guide bushing and a ½-in. router bit, the slots in the jig must be ⅛ in. bigger. Mark out parallel lines for the slots, ⅞ in. apart, based on the reference points you just created. Mark the ends of the slots as well.

7. The best way to proceed now is to make a very simple jig to help you rout the slots. You'll use this interim jig to cut the ⅞-in.-wide slots (see "Making the Interim Slot Jig").

8. Lay the interim jig over one of the marked slot locations on the side-panel jig and clamp it into place. Use a flush-trimming bit in a router to cut the slot all the way through the side-panel jig. Make sure to do this with the jig either propped up off the bench or hanging over the edge so you don't rout into the benchtop.

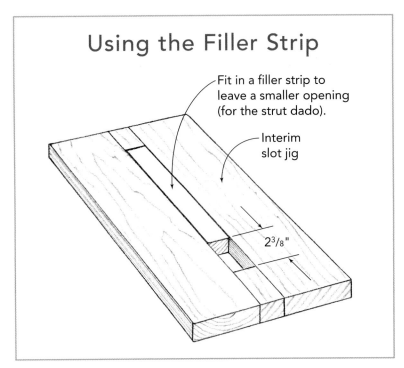

Using the Filler Strip

Fit in a filler strip to leave a smaller opening (for the strut dado).

Interim slot jig

2³/₈"

PHOTO A: A filler strip can be inserted in the interim dado jig to rout the short slot for the strut.

9. Don't worry about the length of the slot for the back of the rocker; it can extend up above where the side panel will end. But you can cut down the 12½-in.-long piece you set aside when making the interim jig to use as a filler when routing the dado for the strut

Cap-Nut Locations

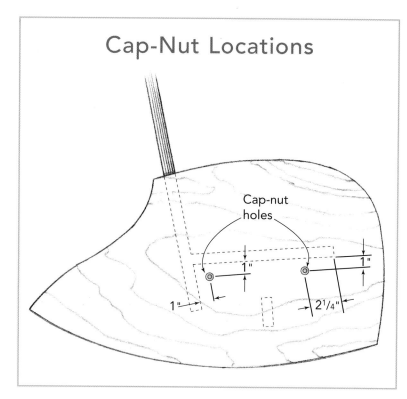

Cap-nut holes

1"

1"

1"

1"

2¼"

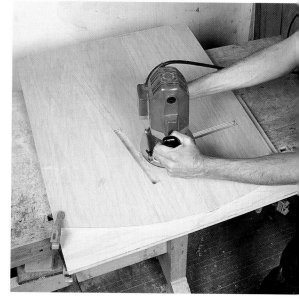

PHOTO B: The dadoes in the side panels are easy to rout, and they come out in exactly the right place if you use the dado jig.

Transferring the Shape

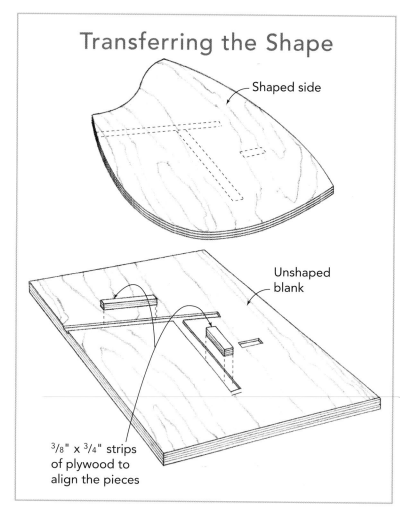

Shaped side

Unshaped blank

³⁄₈" x ³⁄₄" strips of plywood to align the pieces

underneath the seat. This dado should be exactly 2¼ in. long; cut the filler strip so it will make a slot that is 2⅜ in. long in the side-panel jig—⅛ in. will be lost when you rout the dadoes (see **Photo A** on p. 97 and "Using the Filler Strip" on p. 97).

10. Locate and drill two holes which you will use to transfer the positions of the cap-nut holes (see "Cap-Nut Locations").

11. Now cut and smooth the shape of the rocker that you marked originally. I sawed the shape on the bandsaw and sanded the curve smooth and fair. The jig is now finished. Time to move on to making the rocker.

Making the Side Panels

1. Cut the side panel blanks to rough size as given in the cut list.

2. Clamp a panel blank underneath the side-panel jig so that it is flush with the reference edge of the jig. The bottom of the blank should be sticking out beyond the jig about 1 in.

3. Rout the dadoes using a router with a ⅝-in. guide bushing and a ½-in. straight bit. The dadoes should all be the same: ³⁄₁₆ in. to ¼ in. deep. While the boards are still clamped together, mark the curve of the rocker and the cap-nut hole locations onto the blank (see **Photo B**).

4. Now flip the side-panel jig over and clamp it with the same reference edge flush with the edge of the other side-panel blank. Rout the dadoes on this blank. You do not need to mark the rocker curve on this blank, since you will later transfer over the shape of the first panel.

5. Draw a grid of 1-in. squares on the routed side of the first side panel blank.

6. Create the shape of the upper part of the side panel by working square by square from "The Side-Panel Pattern" on p. 94 until you are satisfied with the overall look.

7. Cut the side panel to shape and smooth carefully to the lines. The rocker should be smooth and even, with no bumps or flats.

8. Now transfer the shape over to the other side-panel blank. Use a couple of narrow rippings of ¾-in. plywood fit into the corresponding dadoes to align the two halves before drawing the lines (see "Transferring the Shape"). This will ensure symmetry to the sides. Cut and smooth the second side panel.

9. Round over the edges of both panels with a ¼-in. roundover bit.

10. Drill the two ¹¹⁄₃₂-in. holes for the cap nuts in each side panel at the locations marked from the side-panel jig.

Making the Seat

1. Cut the seat blank to dimensions given in the cut list. Measure 1⁹⁄₁₆ in. in from both sides of the blank to get the dimensions of the back of the seat. Then draw lines from these marks to the front corners.

2. Bandsaw the sides of the seat to the lines.

3. Rout the front edge, both top and bottom, with a ¼-in. roundover bit.

4. The back edge of the seat needs a bevel, but this must wait until you are working on the back.

Making the Back

Both sides of the back are beveled at the same angle as the seat taper. The back also

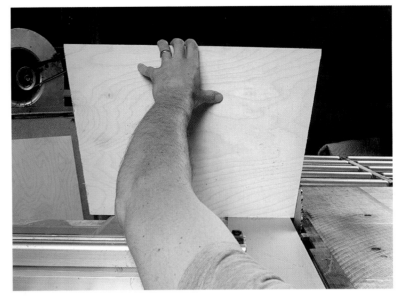

PHOTO C: The seat can be used to set the angle of the table saw blade for all of the bevel cuts on the rocker.

has a dado for the back edge of the seat to slip into as well as some decorative shaping.

1. Set the bevel angle for the back on the table saw using the seat itself as a guide (see **Photo C**).

2. Bevel only one edge of the back for now.

3. You need to determine the location of the dado that will accept the back edge of the seat. The first step is to round over the bottom edges of the back with a ¼-in. roundover bit.

4. Hold up the back with the beveled edge in the back dado of the appropriate side panel (the back should lean toward the back of the chair). Slide the back to the bottom of the dado. Now mark where the seat dado intersects the back (see **Photo D** on p. 100). This marks the location of the seat dado in the back panel.

5. Cut the dado in the back for the seat. Although this dado should be angled, the saw blade on my table saw tilts the wrong way, and it seemed rather cumbersome to set up the cut. So I cut the dado with the blade at 90 degrees and checked the fit of the seat in the dado. No problem. It hardly matters at all that the angle isn't there. And it is easier.

6. Hold the back up in the same side panel as before. Take the seat and hold it up in

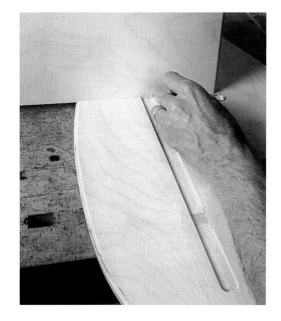

PHOTO D: Locate the dado in the back panel with the panel held in position on the side panel. The dado goes where the seat dado intersects the back.

place as well. Take note of how much wood must be removed from the back edge of the seat so it will fit into place, then mark the back edge.

7. Cut the back edge of the seat with the blade reset to the angle of the seat taper (use the seat as your angle reference once again). Set up for the cut carefully so that the top of the seat ends up longer than the bottom.

8. Now you need the exact width of the back. Hold the seat up in the dado in the back. Align the beveled edge of the back with the edge of the seat. Mark the opposite side. Cut the bevel on this side of the back. Be sure that the bevel angles the correct way. The back panel tapers toward the rear; the edges are not parallel.

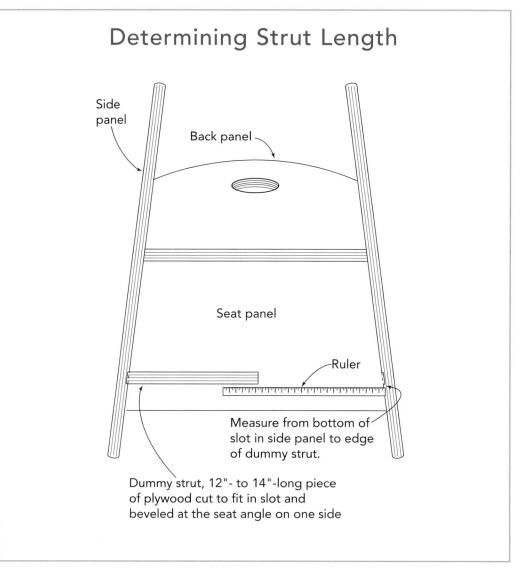

Determining Strut Length

Side panel

Back panel

Seat panel

Ruler

Measure from bottom of slot in side panel to edge of dummy strut.

Dummy strut, 12"- to 14"-long piece of plywood cut to fit in slot and beveled at the seat angle on one side

9. Mark and cut the curves on the top and bottom of the back. Both of these curves are the same: a 30-in. radius. You can use the bottom of one of the side panels as a pattern to mark them out.

10. Rout an oval or a slot in the back panel for decoration. Note that the oval makes a very convenient handle for dragging the chair around. I made up a jig for the oval cutout from a scrap of plywood with a 5⅜-in. by 3⅜-in. oval cut in it. The slot can be cut with the interim jig you made earlier. Cut either decoration with a router with a ⅝-in. guide bushing and a ½-in. straight bit.

Making the Strut

The strut makes it possible to assemble the rocker with a threaded rod and cap nuts. It is simple to make.

1. Cut a strip of plywood to the dimensions given in the cut list.

2. You'll have to clamp all of the other parts of the rocker together to determine the exact length of the strut. Clamp across the back of the chair above the seat. Then measure the distance from the front of the slot on one side to the front of the slot on the other. A 12-in. ruler and a 6-in. ruler used together can get the length. You can also make up a dummy strut from a 1¾-in. by 12-in.- to 14-in.-long scrap of plywood with the seat angle cut on one end. Fit it into one of the strut slots and measure from the end of this piece to the bottom of the dado opposite. Add the two lengths to get the measurement (see "Determining Strut Length").

3. With the saw still tilted (or reset to the seat angle), cut the ends of the strut at the same angle used for cutting the sides of the back.

4. Round over the long edges of the strut with a ¼-in. roundover bit.

Putting It All Together

There is no glue used on this chair. Instead, the chair is held together with two lengths of threaded rod and four cap nuts (see **Photo E**). The cap nuts are usually used in conjunction with connector bolts, but they work perfectly well with ¼-20 threaded rod.

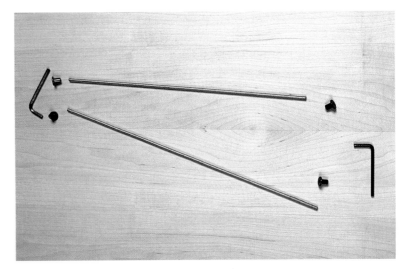

PHOTO E: This combination of hardware used to hold the rocker together is unconventional, but I found it all at my local hardware store.

Tension from the rods and cap nuts holds the seat and back panels securely in the side panels (see "The Threaded Rods" on p. 103). The only complication to this otherwise simple solution is that the rocker side panels are not parallel. The holes (with shallow counterbores) for the connector nuts need to be drilled at an angle so that they can be tightened onto the threaded rods. The process starts with drilling these holes.

Drilling the angled holes

The first step in drilling the angled holes is to make a simple angled drilling platform (see "Making the Angled Drilling Platform" on p. 102).

1. The seat angle provides the angle needed for the drilling platform. Make two identical wedges for the platform out of a piece of wood, roughly 1 in. thick by 3 in. wide by 11 in. long. Align the front edge of the seat panel with the end of this wedge blank and trace the angle of the side of the seat panel onto the blank.

2. Cut a wedge out of the blank, smooth the sawn edge, and use this wedge to mark out a second wedge. Cut and smooth this wedge to match the first.

3. Screw a 12-in.-square piece of ¾-in.-thick plywood to the two wedges.

Making the Angled Drilling Platform

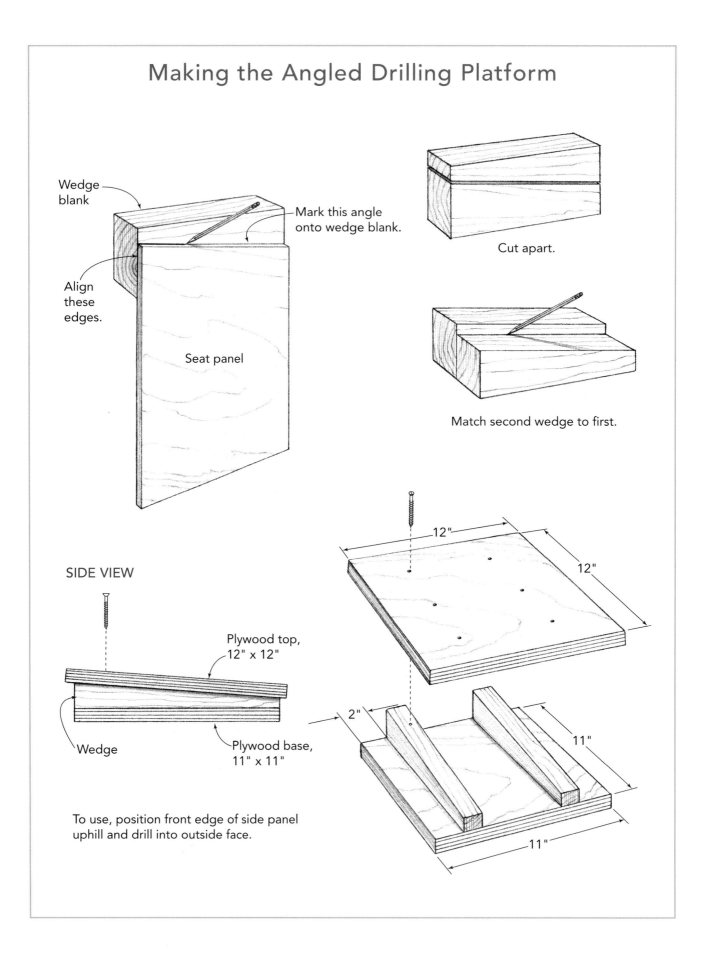

Wedge blank

Mark this angle onto wedge blank.

Align these edges.

Seat panel

Cut apart.

Match second wedge to first.

SIDE VIEW

Plywood top, 12" x 12"

Wedge

Plywood base, 11" x 11"

To use, position front edge of side panel uphill and drill into outside face.

12"

12"

2"

11"

11"

The Threaded Rods

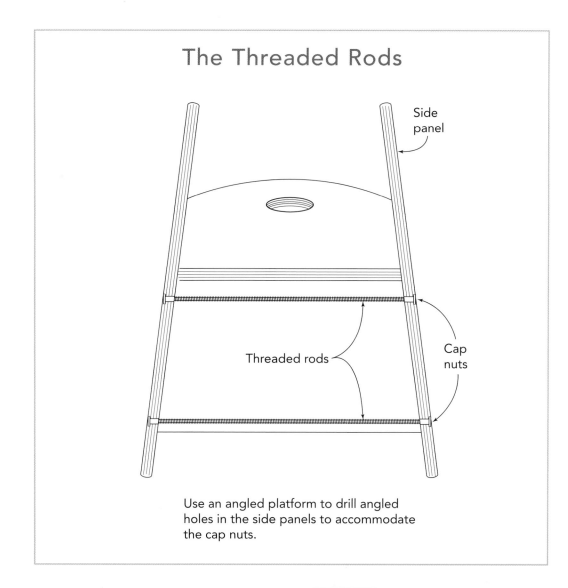

Side panel

Threaded rods

Cap nuts

Use an angled platform to drill angled holes in the side panels to accommodate the cap nuts.

4. Attaching a piece of plywood to the underside of the wedges will make it easier to clamp the angled platform to the drill-press table.
5. Clamp the angled platform to the drill-press table with the angle running sideways.
6. On the outside of each of the side panels draw a line through the two marks for the cap-nut holes. This line should remain parallel to the edge of the angled platform when drilling the holes in a side.
7. Drill a shallow ¾-in. counterbore for the flange of each of the cap nuts first. Drill only until you have a complete hole; it will still be very shallow on one side. Then drill a 9mm or a ⅜-in. hole through the center of the counterbore for the body of each of the nuts (see **Photo F**).

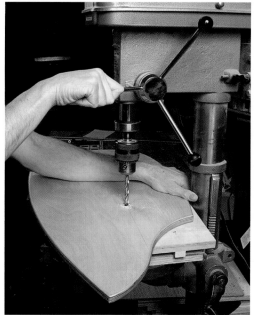

PHOTO F: With the angled platform clamped in place on the drill press, it's easy to drill the holes for the cap nuts at the proper angle. Note that the line through the cap-nut holes is parallel to the edge of the angled platform and that the front of the side panel is uphill.

PHOTOS G AND H: Assembling the rocker can be frustrating without help. It makes sense to do it on a blanket or a piece of cardboard in case something slips apart.

PHOTO I: Slip the threaded rod with one of the cap nuts all the way through the holes in one side and mark where the rod comes out the counterbore on the other side panel of the rocker.

Cutting the threaded rod to length

1. Put the rocker together. You may want an assistant or a clamp or two to help hold things together while you measure for the threaded rod (see **Photos G** and **H**).

2. Thread one of the cap nuts all the way onto the end of the rod, and insert it into a hole on one side and then through the hole in the other side. Mark where the rod comes out of the hole, flush with the bottom of the counterbore (see **Photo I**).

3. Cut the rod ¼ in. shorter than the length you marked. File the rough edges and check to be sure you can thread the nut onto the cut end.

4. Repeat the same process for the other set of holes, using the remaining section of rod.

5. Now assemble the chair with the threaded rod in place.

PHOTO J: Tighten up the cap nuts with a pair of Allen wrenches.

6. Tighten the cap nuts (see **Photo J**). The rocker should hold together tightly (if not, check to see if you need to cut a little more off of the threaded rods). You can test the chair now if you want.

Finishing

I chose an oil-and-wax finish for a natural look on one of the rockers and brightly colored paint for the other. Lacquer or shellac is also a good option, although paint, lacquer, or shellac on the bottoms of the rockers will probably rub off as the chair is dragged around. Sand all parts thoroughly, especially the edges, before applying any finish. Wait for the finish to dry completely before reassembling the rocker. Then put it into use.

TIP

It's easy to cut threaded rod with a hacksaw. It's also very easy to mangle the threads so they are unusable. Remember that you need good threads on only the last ½ in. of either end of the rod. Clamp somewhere else when you're cutting.

MARBLE CHAIR

IT IS HARD TO CONVEY IN A PHOTO exactly what this chair does. It may be obvious from the name and the basic shape that the back of the chair incorporates a marble "slider" track. But the chair does more than roll marbles. It fascinates kids. It also entertains adults. It makes wonderful noises as the marbles roll and drop down. It makes people smile.

One of the things I did to prepare for writing this book was to spend some time in my daughter's kindergarten class talking to the students about chairs. The children were amazingly forthcoming and even created a "chair museum" of models and drawings that they did. I might have been hoping to steal a chair idea for this book from them—which didn't happen—but instead I was inspired to come up with two chair designs, the better of which is this marble chair. When I first brought this chair into class, it caused quite a stir (an understatement, to be sure). It still generates excitement.

One little secret about this project; it is a real chair. But never mind if you haven't done one before. Plunge ahead and make it. You won't regret it.

MARBLE CHAIR

TAKE THE TIME TO MAKE SURE you understand the angles throughout this project. You'll realize that once you've made up the necessary chair wedge, all of the cutting, joinery, and drilling can be done without much additional effort. Note that many of the dimensions for this project come from work already done.

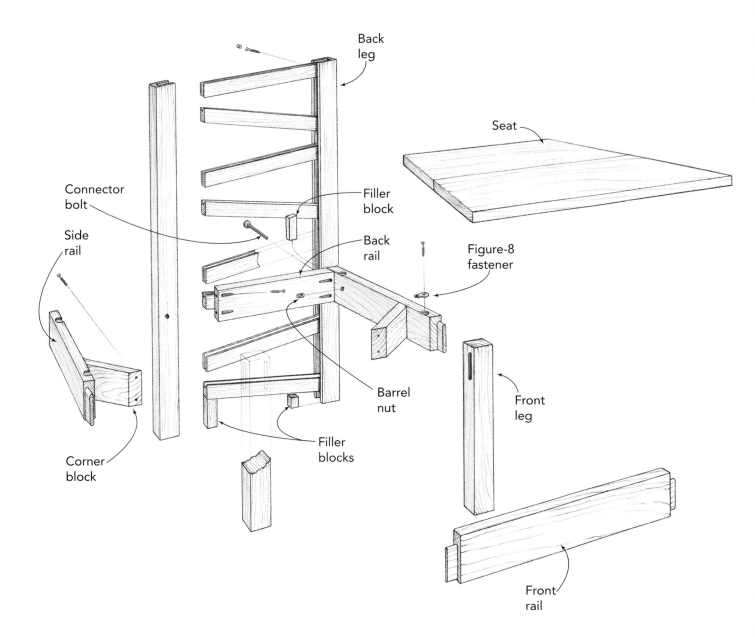

Back leg

Seat

Connector bolt

Filler block

Side rail

Back rail

Figure-8 fastener

Barrel nut

Corner block

Filler blocks

Front leg

Front rail

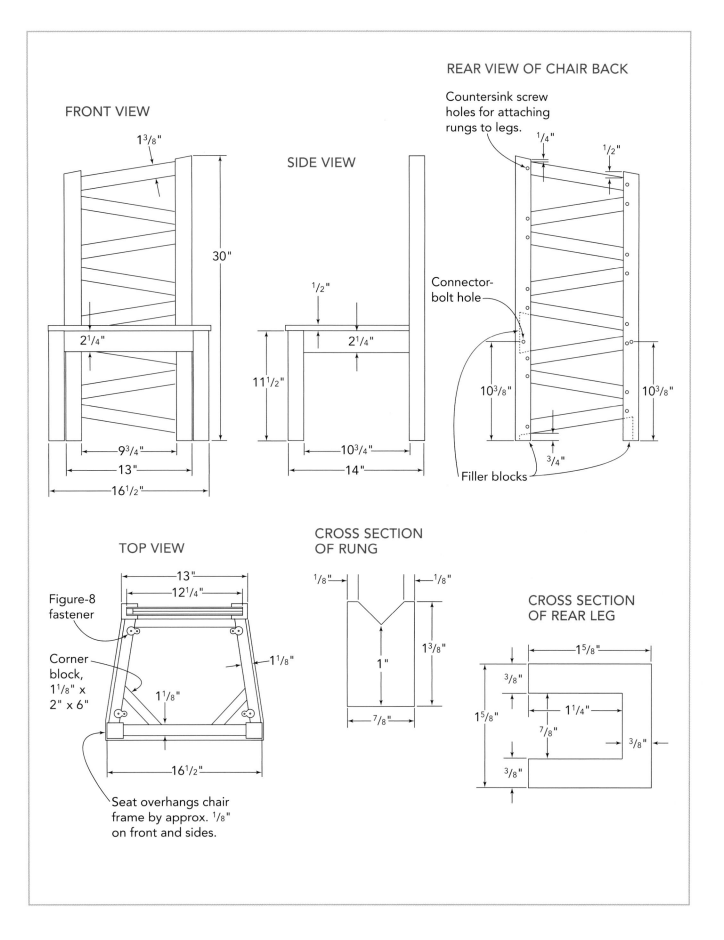

FRONT VIEW

$1^3/_8$"

30"

$2^1/_4$"

$9^3/_4$"

13"

$16^1/_2$"

SIDE VIEW

$1/_2$"

$2^1/_4$"

$11^1/_2$"

$10^3/_4$"

14"

REAR VIEW OF CHAIR BACK

Countersink screw holes for attaching rungs to legs.

$1/_4$"

$1/_2$"

Connector-bolt hole

$10^3/_8$"

$10^3/_8$"

$3/_4$"

Filler blocks

TOP VIEW

Figure-8 fastener

13"

$12^1/_4$"

Corner block, $1^1/_8$" x 2" x 6"

$1^1/_8$"

$1^1/_8$"

$16^1/_2$"

Seat overhangs chair frame by approx. $1/_8$" on front and sides.

CROSS SECTION OF RUNG

$1/_8$"

$1/_8$"

$1^3/_8$"

1"

$7/_8$"

CROSS SECTION OF REAR LEG

$1^5/_8$"

$3/_8$"

$1^1/_4$"

$1^5/_8$"

$7/_8$"

$3/_8$"

$3/_8$"

$3/_8$"

CUT LIST FOR MARBLE CHAIR

2	Rear legs	1⅝" x 1⅝" x 30"
2	Front legs	1⅝" x 1⅝" x 11½"
8	Back rungs	⅞" x 1⅜" x 12½" (rough length)
1	Front rail	1⅛" x 2¼" x 15¼" (rough length)
2	Side rails	1⅛" x 2¼" x 12" (rough length)
1	Back rail	1⅛" x 2¼" x 11" (rough length)
1	Seat	½" x 12½" x 16¾" (minimum size)
2	Corner blocks	1⅛" x 2" x 6"
Hardware		
2	Connector bolts	¼-20 x 3½"
2	Barrel nuts	¼-20
4	Figure-8 fasteners	
28	Screws	#6 x 1¼"*
4	Screws	#6 x 1"**
4	Pan-head screws	#6 x½"***
4	Glides for leg bottoms	
	Marbles	

*For assembling the back and attaching the corner blocks.
**For attaching the figure-8 fasteners to the side rails.
***For attaching the seat to the figure-8 fasteners.

PHOTO A: Be patient when cutting the large dado in the back legs. Trying to hog away all of the wood in one pass is dangerous.

I HAVE TRIED TO KEEP the complicated joinery on this chair to a minimum. And although there are a lot of angles all over the chair, they're almost all the same angle, which makes things much easier.

Making the Back

The back is where all of the action is on this chair, although it is not very difficult to make. And it's a good place to start.

Preparing the legs

1. Mill the stock for all four legs.

2. Cut the front legs to length and set them aside. Cut the back legs at least 30 in. long for now.

3. There is a lot of wood to cut away on the insides of the back legs. Set up to cut the ⅞-in.-wide by 1¼-in.-deep dado centered on the leg (see **Photo A**). Cut this dado in mul-

PHOTO B: Use the same fence setting for both of the cuts to make the V-groove. Turn the rung stock around for the second cut. It's important for safe handling on the saw to retain the narrow flats on either side of the V-groove.

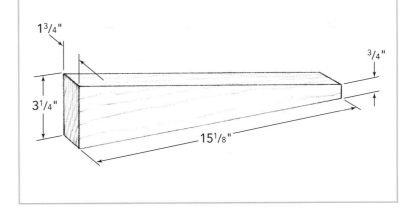

PHOTO C: The chair wedge ensures that all of your rung cuts are the same, but it also will do much more throughout the project.

tiple small passes, raising the dado head between passes. The results will cleaner and the process safer than trying to cut it all at once.

Preparing the rungs

The rungs are much easier to make if you shape them in long strips and then cut them to length. Don't get carried away though; a 38-in. or 50-in. length (equal to three or four strips) is manageable and safe.

1. Mill up the rung stock to its approximate width and thickness. Don't go just by the numbers here. It pays to start with rung stock that's a little on the thick side; then work down to a snug fit in the rear-leg dadoes. Make sure you have enough stock for all eight rungs, plus two or three extra. You'll use some of this stock later, both for testing and for filling in the dado in specific places.

2. Cut the V-groove for the marbles on the table saw with the blade tilted to 45 degrees. This will take two passes, one from each end of the rung stock (see **Photo B**). Use some of the extra rung stock to set up the cut (see p. 109 for details).

3. Make up the chair wedge (see "Making the Chair Wedge") to help you cut the rungs at the proper angle. You could easily set the

---

Making the Chair Wedge

If you make the wedge 1³/₄" thick now, you can use it to cut not only the rungs but also the side rails and the side-rail tenons.

1³/₄"

3¹/₄"

³/₄"

15¹/₈"

---

miter guide to the proper angle, but you'll need the wedge later for a whole variety of other cuts, so it pays to make the wedge.

4. Secure the wedge to your miter guide and make the initial cut on each of the pieces of rung stock. Then screw a stop to the wedge so you can cut all of the rungs to exactly the same size. Cut the rungs (see **Photo C**).

Notching the Rungs

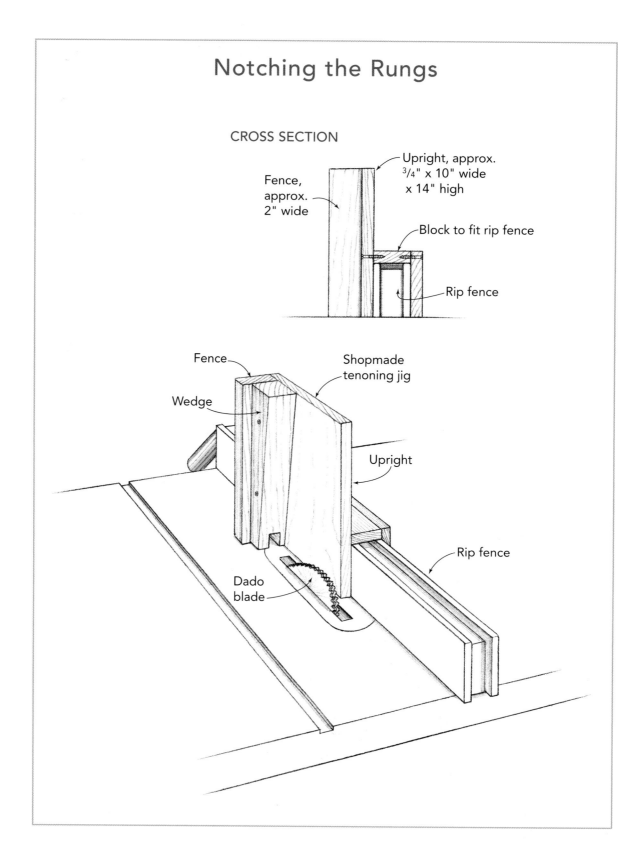

CROSS SECTION

Fence, approx. 2" wide

Upright, approx. 3/4" x 10" wide x 14" high

Block to fit rip fence

Rip fence

Fence

Shopmade tenoning jig

Wedge

Upright

Dado blade

Rip fence

5. Now remove the wedge from the miter guide and attach it to either a purchased or a shopmade tenoning jig (see "Notching the Rungs"), with the narrow end of the wedge down. This will enable you to hold the rungs securely upright with the angled end flat on the saw table when you cut the marble drop slots.

6. Set up a dado blade to cut $^{21}\!/_{32}$ in. wide and $^{21}\!/_{32}$ in. deep. Since most dado sets won't cut $^{21}\!/_{32}$ in. in one pass, you may have to cut a narrower dado and then shift the tenoning jig over to complete the cut. Be sure the dado is perfectly centered in the thickness of the rungs. Clamp a rung into place and cut the marble drop slot (see **Photo D**). Check that a marble will fit—most marbles are a little more than $^{5}\!/_{8}$ in. in diameter. Repeat this for six more rungs. The bottom rung does not get a slot, so the marbles won't fall out onto the floor (where adults would step on them and get angry at me). Be sure to save the wedge.

Assembling the back

It's not easy to get all eight rungs into the slots in the back legs in the correct places and then hold them in position while you drill pilot holes and screw them into place. The best way to do this is to make up an assembly jig (see "Making the Assembly Jig" on p. 114). It takes a little while to build, but this jig makes assembly simple. You're on your own if you try to put the chair all together without it.

1. Fit the legs and rungs together on the assembly jig, with the rungs inserted into the dadoes in the legs. Clamp if necessary to hold things in place.

2. Drill the appropriate size pilot holes.

3. Drive all of the screws into the pilot holes.

Plugging the pilot holes

1. Cut wooden plugs to fill all of the pilot holes in the legs.

2. Glue the plugs in place

3. Trim the plugs off flush with a saw or a chisel and sand the back of the legs smooth.

PHOTO D: You may have to cut the $^{21}\!/_{32}$-in. slot in two passes. Cut all seven rungs at one setting; then shift the jig over to cut the second pass.

Adding filler blocks

There are three places where you need to add filler blocks in the dadoed leg: the bottoms of both legs and the area where one of the connector bolts goes through the leg to join to the side rail (see p. 108).

1. Cut stock to fill the dado in the legs. You can use the extra rail stock if it fits exactly or mill up some new wood.

2. Rip the fillers to exactly the depth of the dado.

3. Use the chair wedge to cut the top of the filler pieces at the correct angle (see **Photo E** on p. 116). You must leave at least $^{1}\!/_{2}$ in. between the third rail up and the filler that goes above it so the marbles will be able to fit through.

4. When each piece fits in its spot, glue and clamp it in place.

MAKING THE ASSEMBLY JIG

1. Start by cutting the ¾-in. plywood to size for the base.

2. Next, you have to make seven identical wedges. Fortunately, only the first wedge must be carefully laid out; the rest can be duplicated easily from that one. Cut a piece of scrap wood ¾ in. to 1 in. thick by 4 in. wide by 9¾ in. long. Draw a line down the center of the piece the long way and mark out the wide end of the wedge on this end, 1¹⁵⁄₁₆ in. to either side of the centerline (or 3⅞ in. overall, centered on the piece).

3. Now you can use the chair wedge you made earlier to draw the correct angle. Line up the wide bottom edge of the chair wedge with the marked end of the assembly-jig wedge blank, so that the slanted side of the chair wedge is on one of the marks on the jig blank. Trace out the taper. Now flip over the chair wedge and mark the taper for the other side of the jig blank.

4. Cut out and carefully smooth the assembly-jig wedge to the lines.

5. Now you need to make six more wedges identical to the first. It's easy if you use the first wedge as a pattern and flush-trim the others. Flush-trimming can be done with a router, but in this case it's simpler on the table saw with an L-shaped fence attached to your rip fence. Align the L-shaped fence directly over the blade on the saw. If you screw the first wedge on top of a slightly oversize blank, you can run the pattern wedge against the L-shaped fence and the saw will cut the blank to the exact same shape and size. After a few cuts, you should shut down the saw and check to make sure the cut-offs are not accumulating underneath the fence. Cut the remaining wedges.

6. To assemble the jig, clamp a leg along one side of the plywood, flush with the edge. Measure up from the bottom of the plywood to locate the first wedge. Butt it up to the leg; then clamp it down and screw it into place. Use a rung with a strip of masking tape on it (to give you a little clearance for when you actually assemble the back) to help position the next wedge. Clamp and screw it into place, then add the rest of the wedges in the same manner.

The completed chair back simply lifts off the assembly jig.

DUPLICATING THE WEDGES

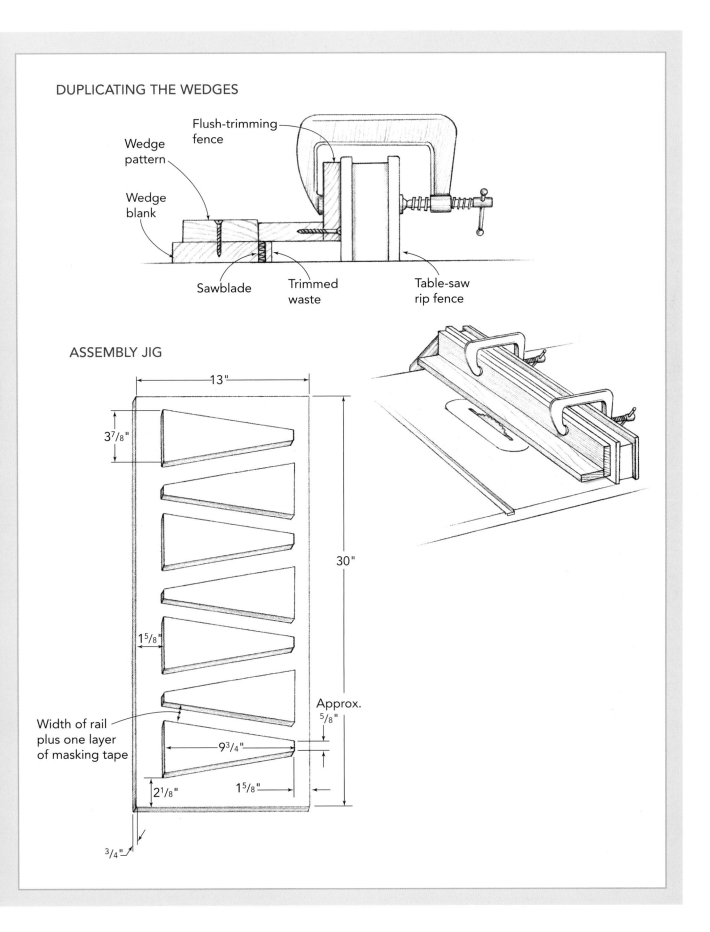

Flush-trimming fence

Wedge pattern

Wedge blank

Sawblade

Trimmed waste

Table-saw rip fence

ASSEMBLY JIG

13"

3⁷/₈"

30"

1⁵/₈"

Approx. ⁵/₈"

Width of rail plus one layer of masking tape

9³/₄"

2¹/₈"

1⁵/₈"

³/₄"

PHOTO E: The filler blocks at the bottom of the legs are necessary for strengthening the leg at this crucial point.

Drilling for the connector bolts

1. Lay out the locations for the connector-bolt holes in the back legs. The holes must go through the filler block on one side and a rung (but not its V-groove) on the other side. Adjust the height of the holes (even asymmetrically), if necessary.

2. Drill the ¼-in. connector-bolt holes through the back legs.

Trimming the tops

The chair wedge is used once again for cutting off the tops of the legs.

1. Mark out the tops of the legs as shown on p. 108.

2. Set the chair wedge against the miter guide on the table saw and place the back assembly against it.

3. Cut one leg off. Then reset and cut the other leg at the proper place.

Making the Front and Sides of the Chair

The rest of the chair has far fewer parts, but don't plan on rushing through this segment of the construction. There may be some unfamiliar stuff here, and you should take the time to understand what to do before

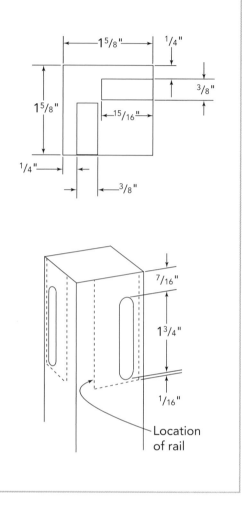

Location of rail

you plunge in. Once you are clear on what goes on, nothing is all that hard. If you want a much more thorough discussion of chairmaking (complete with a different child's chair), see my book *Chairmaking and Design* (The Taunton Press, 1997).

Preparing the front legs

The front legs should already be milled. All that's left to do is to mortise the legs for the front and side rails.

1. Lay out the mortise locations based on the "Front-Leg Mortise Layout."

2. Cut the mortises ¹⁵⁄₁₆ in. deep, using a plunge router and the mortising block shown on p. 12.

Side-Rail Layout

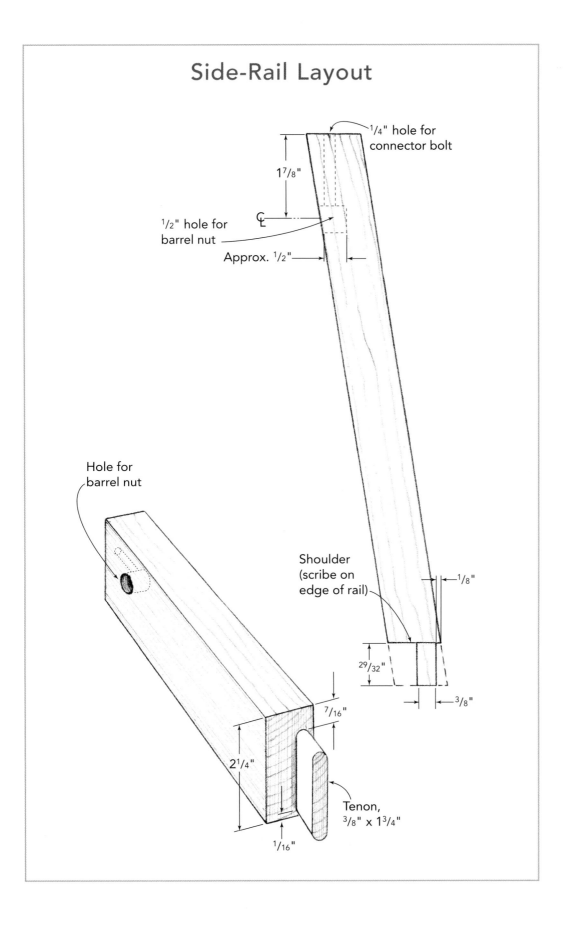

¼" hole for
connector bolt

1⁷/₈"

½" hole for
barrel nut

Approx. ½"

Hole for
barrel nut

Shoulder
(scribe on
edge of rail)

⅛"

29/32"

³/₈"

7/16"

2¼"

Tenon,
³/₈" x 1³/₄"

1/16"

Angled Tenons

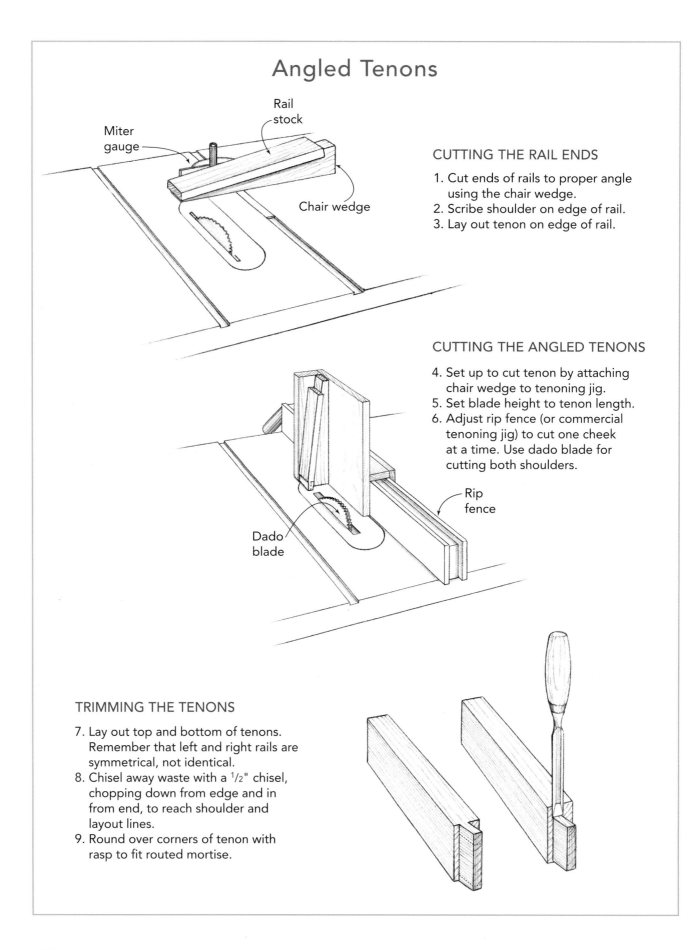

Miter gauge

Rail stock

Chair wedge

CUTTING THE RAIL ENDS

1. Cut ends of rails to proper angle using the chair wedge.
2. Scribe shoulder on edge of rail.
3. Lay out tenon on edge of rail.

CUTTING THE ANGLED TENONS

4. Set up to cut tenon by attaching chair wedge to tenoning jig.
5. Set blade height to tenon length.
6. Adjust rip fence (or commercial tenoning jig) to cut one cheek at a time. Use dado blade for cutting both shoulders.

Rip fence

Dado blade

TRIMMING THE TENONS

7. Lay out top and bottom of tenons. Remember that left and right rails are symmetrical, not identical.
8. Chisel away waste with a 1/2" chisel, chopping down from edge and in from end, to reach shoulder and layout lines.
9. Round over corners of tenon with rasp to fit routed mortise.

Preparing the side rails

Mill the wood for the rails to size and include enough for two extra rails. You'll use one to test out your tenon-cutting setup and it's always nice to have a spare around. The side rails are the crux of the matter. Up front, there is an angled tenon to cut. Fortunately, an angled tenon is no more difficult to cut than a straight one—if you use a wedge to hold the rail at the correct angle. And we've already made up that wedge; the chair wedge you made up earlier works just fine here, too. This process winds up being easier than cutting an angled mortise and a straight tenon with a skewed shoulder.

1. Crosscut three side rails to length (the two you'll use plus one for testing the tenon setup) and at the proper angle (see "Side-Rail Layout" on p. 117). The chair wedge works for this, too.

2. Now set up the chair wedge by attaching it to the side of your tenoning jig. This will angle the rail from side to side, which is different from how you angled the jig to cut the marble drop.

3. Lay out the tenon location carefully on one of the rails.

4. The best way to cut the angled tenons is to use a tenoning jig with a wedge and a dado blade on the table saw (see "Angled Tenons"). This way you cut both the tenon cheek and the shoulder at the same time, and they are at right angles and should line up perfectly from one side to the other. Cut one side of the tenon on all three rails; then set up to cut the other side of the tenon. Cut a test tenon first, and check to see that it will fit snugly in the mortise by inserting a corner. Adjust the setup, if necessary, and then cut the two final rails (see **Photo F**).

5. Cut the top and bottom of the tenon using a ½-in. chisel. Chisel down from the edge of the tenon; then remove the waste by chiseling in from the end. Remove a small amount and repeat until you reach the shoulder and the layout lines.

6. Round over the ends of the tenons with a rasp to fit the rounded ends of the mortises.

7. Fit the tenons carefully in the mortises. The fit should be snug but not so tight that

TIP

You don't need to lay out both rails, because the setup for cutting the rails will be the same.

PHOTO F: An angled tenon is no more difficult to cut than a straight one, once you have the wedge attached to the tenoning jig. Note that the tenon is angled but the shoulders are perpendicular to the tenon.

PHOTO G: The rabbeting plane is designed for fitting tenons. You can also use a rasp or sandpaper on a block. Whatever your tool, be careful not to taper or round over the face of the tenon.

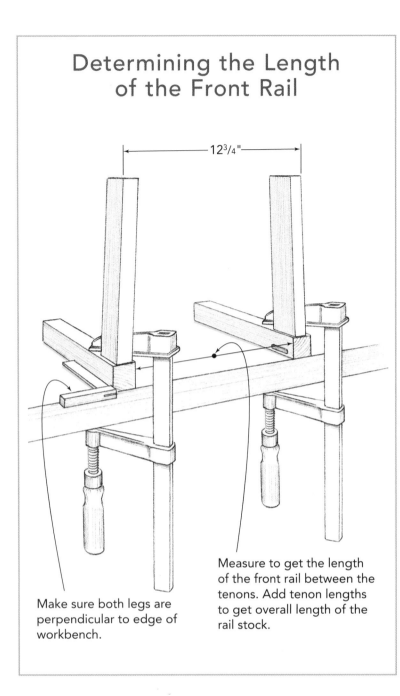

Determining the Length of the Front Rail

12³/4"

Make sure both legs are perpendicular to edge of workbench.

Measure to get the length of the front rail between the tenons. Add tenon lengths to get overall length of the rail stock.

PHOTO H: The connector-bolt hole in the back leg guides the drill into the back of the side rail.

3. Cut the tenons to size, round over the corners, and fit the tenons carefully to the mortises.

Gluing up the front legs and rail

1. Insert (without glue) small scraps of ⅜-in.-thick wood into the mortises for the side rails. These will prevent the side-rail mortises from getting crushed when you clamp the legs to the front rail.
2. Spread glue in the front-rail mortises and very lightly on the front rail tenons. Insert the tenons into the mortises and clamp.

Attaching the Front and the Rear

1. Insert the side-rail tenons into the front legs without glue and clamp this assembly to the back assembly. It's not hard to put the front and back together so the side rails are parallel to the floor, but you might want a hand keeping the clamps away from the connector-bolt hole in the back.

you need to force the joint together with a mallet. If the fit is too loose, you can glue a thin shim onto one side of the tenon and refit the tenon with a shoulder plane after the glue dries (see **Photo G** on p. 119).

Preparing the front rail

1. Measure the length of the front rail between the tenons (see "Determining the Length of the Front Rail").
2. Lay out the tenon locations on both ends of the front rail.

PHOTO I: The holes for the barrel nuts don't need to be very deep, since the connector bolt will be close to the inside face of the rail. Be sure you don't drill through the rail!

2. Drill through the connector-bolt holes in the back as far as you can into the side rails. You may have to drill deeper after you unclamp (see **Photo H**).

3. Disassemble and drill for the barrel nuts on the inside of the side rails using the chair wedge to hold the rail at the proper angle (see **Photo I**). Use a drill press with a depth stop to be sure you locate the holes accurately.

4. Now you can glue the side rails to the front leg-and-rail assembly. This is easiest to do if you clamp down onto a workbench (see "Clamping the Leg-and-Rail Assembly"), or you could use a thick board that is at least as long as the front-leg assembly. The important thing is to get clamping pressure right at the joint, perpendicular to the plane of the shoulder.

5. When this assembly is dry, you can bolt on the back assembly. You don't need to use glue.

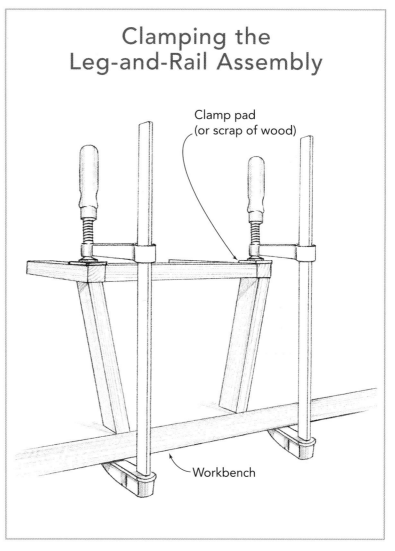

Clamping the Leg-and-Rail Assembly

Clamp pad (or scrap of wood)

Workbench

Adding the back rail

With all the ramp rungs joining the two back legs, the back rail doesn't have much structural significance, but the chair looks wrong without it. Fortunately, it's easy to make.

1. Cut one end of the back rail at the proper angle using the chair wedge.

2. Hold the rail up against the back legs and mark out the other end so that it will just fit in between the side rails at the back legs. Cut this end using the chair wedge.

3. Drill two pocket-screw holes on the inside face of each end of the rail. Check what length screws you'll need.

4. Hold the rail in position and screw it into place.

PHOTO J: The shallow holes for the figure-8 fasteners have to overlap the inside edge of the rail. Use the fastener itself as a guide in determining how much overlap you need.

Making the Seat

The seat is a simple plank, cut and shaped to fit over the frame of the chair. The grain on the plank runs from side to side, allowing the seat to expand and contract at the front.

Shaping the seat

1. Glue up a plank for the seat ½ in. thick, and at least ½ in. longer and wider than the final seat width and depth. Smooth out the seat plank and the back edge by planing, scraping, and/or sanding.

2. Turn the chair over and place it on the seat blank, positioning the back of the seat flush with the back legs. Draw a line about ⅛ in. away from the front legs on both the front and the sides of the legs. Connect the lines across the front and then draw lines back to the rear leg lines.

3. Cut out the shape on the bandsaw; then smooth to your lines by planing or sanding.

4. Round the front corners of the seat. Then rout a rounded profile on the top edges with a ¼-in. roundover bit and a much smaller radius on the bottom (a ⅛-in. roundover bit, not set to full depth).

Attaching the seat

I used a type of tabletop fastener I call a figure-8 (so named for its shape) to attach the seat to the rails. This allows for expansion and contraction of the seat over the rails. Alternatively, you could drill up through the rails if you make sure to enlarge the holes toward the front, to allow for wood movement.

1. Drill the tops of the rails for the figure-8 fasteners with a ¾-in. Forstner bit. Hold the drill off the edge of the rail a little, to allow room for the fastener to extend off the rail. Drill deep enough to recess the fastener completely in the rail (see **Photo J**).

2. Screw the figure-8 fasteners into place from the top with 1-in. long screws.

3. Place the seat in position; then screw from below into the seat with ½-in. long pan-head screws.

Installing Corner Blocks and Glides

Corner blocks add significantly to the strength of the front leg joints and so to the overall life of the chair. Unfortunately, the chair wedge you've used for just about every other angle doesn't help here. You'll have to lay out the corner blocks from the chair.

PHOTO K: Hold the corner block in place and screw into the front rail and then the side rail.

1. Mill stock for the two corner blocks: 1⅛ in. thick by 2 in. wide by about 14 in. long. If you still have leftover side-rail stock, you can rip that to width.

2. Set the blade on the table saw to the proper angle (see "Corner-Block Layout") and cut two corner blocks about 5½ in. long.

3. Drill pocket holes for screws to attach the corner blocks.

4. Screw the corner blocks into place with whatever length screws will hold them securely to the side rails (see **Photo K**).

5. Attach glides to the bottoms of all four legs. Drill the back legs for the glides, so you don't split the filler blocks when you hammer the glides in.

Finishing

Apply the finish of your choice. Now, find some marbles and have some fun. Once you give the chair to a child you won't have as much time to play with it as you might like.

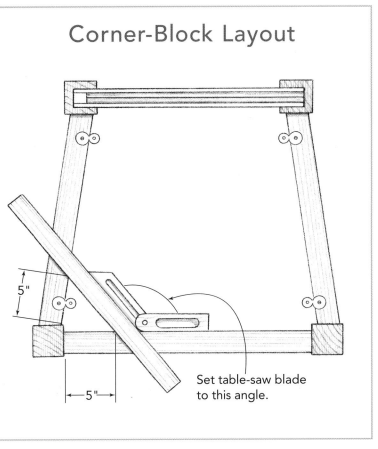

Corner-Block Layout

5"

5"

Set table-saw blade to this angle.

A ROCKING DINOSAUR

I STARTED MAKING ROCKING DINOSAURS when my niece—the first of her generation—was born. I got a little carried away. The dinosaur I built was big enough for my niece, my sister, and my mother to ride on at the same time. I didn't know much about children (or dinosaurs) at the time. The design quickly changed, and over the next few versions not only did I change the scale of the dinosaur but I came up with the idea of a rocking tyrannosaurus. Kids love riding on this dinosaur, but they also like his fierce demeanor. I keep a version in my showroom to occupy children while I talk to their parents about grown-up furniture. I often find the children, especially the little ones, bravely sticking their hands into that toothy mouth.

On a rocking animal that will see some aggressive use (and that means all rocking animals), the rockers should be long enough to prevent tipping, and they should be either laminated or quite thick for strength.

A ROCKING DINOSAUR

THIS ROCKING TYRANNOSAUR is unusual for a rocking animal because of its upright posture. Making a two-legged rocking beast is more difficult than the usual four-legged creature; there is tremendous leverage out at the ends of the rockers. Fortunately, the tail provides the solution. A crosspiece between the rockers at the back of the dinosaur attaches to the tail, and keeps everything strong and stable.

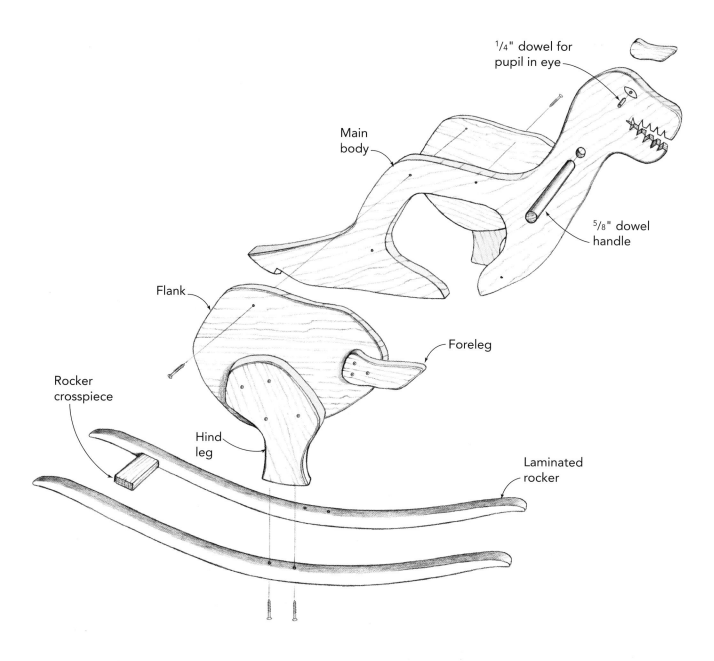

¼" dowel for pupil in eye

Main body

⅝" dowel handle

Flank

Foreleg

Rocker crosspiece

Hind leg

Laminated rocker

Dinosaur Patterns

The parts are shown in position so they can be located properly.

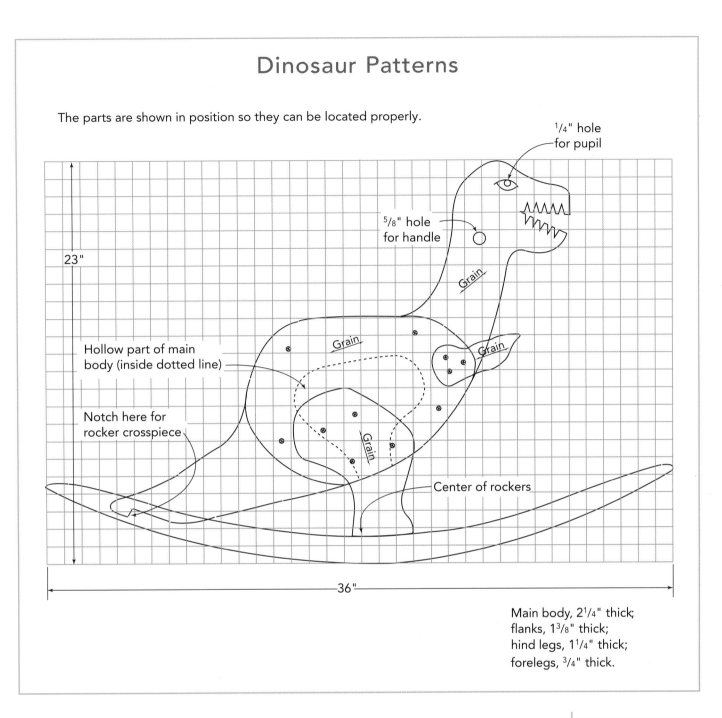

¹/₄" hole for pupil

⁵/₈" hole for handle

23"

Hollow part of main body (inside dotted line)

Notch here for rocker crosspiece

Grain

Grain

Grain

Grain

Center of rockers

36"

Main body, 2¹/₄" thick;
flanks, 1³/₈" thick;
hind legs, 1¹/₄" thick;
forelegs, ³/₄" thick.

THE BODY OF THE DINOSAUR involves lots of bandsaw work and lots of smoothing. To make all this go easier, build the body of the dinosaur out of a wood that is relatively easy to shape (I chose poplar). The rockers call for a different technique—lamination. And for this you should use maple or another hard, strong wood.

Making the Patterns

Start the project by making plywood patterns for the four main parts of the dinosaur's body. These will help you refine the shapes a little and make it easier to lay out the solid-wood blanks more efficiently.

1. Draw a grid of 1-in. squares on a piece of ¼-in. plywood and draw the patterns directly on that (see "Dinosaur Patterns"). Or transfer the patterns to graph paper and either

TIP
You can change the size of the dinosaur if you wish by changing the size of the squares in the grid you transfer the drawing to.

CUT LIST FOR ROCKING DINOSAUR

The Body

1	Main body	2¼" x 11" x 33"
2	Flanks	1⅜" x 10½" x 14"
2	Forelegs	¾" x 2½" x 6"
2	Hind legs	1¼" x 6½" x 10"
2	Dowels (for pupils in the eyes)	¼" x ½"
1	Dowel (for handle)	⅝" x 8½"
	Plywood (for parts patterns)	

The Rockers

22	Strips of maple	⅛" x 1¾" x 43"
1	Crosspiece	¾" x 2½" x 5⁵⁄₁₆"
	Screws	#6 x 1¼
	Screws	#8 x 2
	Screws	#10 x 3
	Plywood, particleboard, or MDF (for laminating forms)	

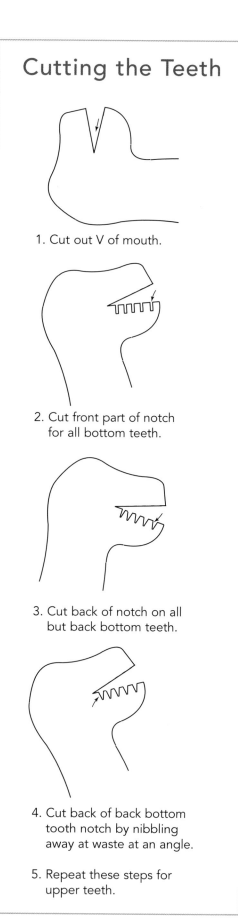

Cutting the Teeth

1. Cut out V of mouth.

2. Cut front part of notch for all bottom teeth.

3. Cut back of notch on all but back bottom teeth.

4. Cut back of back bottom tooth notch by nibbling away at waste at an angle.

5. Repeat these steps for upper teeth.

TIP
Save some of the curved cutoffs to use as support blocks when routing the eyes and as sanding blocks during the smoothing process.

transfer an enlarged copy onto ¼-in. plywood with carbon paper or glue it down to the plywood and cut the plywood right through it. It will help later if you lay out the leg positions on the flank pattern now.

2. Cut out the patterns on the bandsaw. Be careful to stay outside the lines. It will take some maneuvering (or a coping saw) to cut out the teeth in the mouth.

3. Smooth the patterns with sandpaper. Don't be too concerned about achieving perfectly smooth and even curves. Some lumpiness is part of the look. The main body pattern (which includes the head and tail) and the pattern for the two flanks do have to fit together well, however. Smooth the main body pattern first; then smooth the flank pattern so it matches up with the body on both the top and the bottom.

Making the Body

Roughing out the parts
1. Mill or glue up and then smooth the faces of the blanks for the various body parts.

2. Trace the shape of the main body from the plywood pattern onto the main body blank and cut it out on the bandsaw. Be careful to stay outside the lines. Skip the mouth for now.

3. Cut the main V of the mouth (see "Cutting the Teeth").

4. Work carefully when cutting out each of the notches between the teeth. You won't be able to do this with a blade bigger than ¼ in. First cut the side of the V that's closest to the front of the mouth for each of the notches on either the upper or lower jaw (whichever way fits on your bandsaw). Then work on the back side of the Vs. At the very back notch, you won't be able to make a regular cut. Instead, use the blade to nibble away some of the wood, pushing the wood at an angle across the teeth.

5. If you can't cut all of the teeth because there isn't room in the throat of your bandsaw, lay out the teeth on the opposite side of the body and cut from that side as well. Align the pattern carefully with the body (and especially the head) when marking the teeth. If this doesn't work, get out a coping saw and cut the notches by hand.

Smoothing the body parts

There are a number of options for smoothing all of these curves.

1. I usually set up a drum sander for the tighter curves, but the rest of the curves are better done by hand with a spokeshave, scrapers, and sandpaper backed with flat or curved sanding blocks. I tend to use a combination of all of these methods (see **Photos A** and **B**).

2. However you start the process, you should finish by working up to 220-grit sandpaper on sanding blocks.

Cutting the main body details

1. Mark out the eyes; then rout with a ⅛-in. bit. Rout freehand close to the lines and then cut to the final shape with chisels and gouges.

2. Drill ¼-in. holes about ½-in. deep for the pupils and then insert a ¼-in. dowel with the end rounded over (see **Photo C** on p. 130).

PHOTO A: A spoke-shave works well for smoothing both the convex and the shallower concave sections of the body parts.

PHOTO B: Tighter curves can be sanded with a sanding block that roughly matches the curve to be smoothed.

PHOTO C: To make the pupils, tap ¼-in. dowels, which have the ends rounded over, into the holes in the eyes. Tap until only the rounded part of the dowel is exposed.

PHOTO D: With the shape of the leg cut out of it, the flank pattern helps locate the legs in the same place on both sides of the dinosaur.

Don't use mushroom plugs for this, since they tend to work out of their holes and can pose a choking hazard. Cut out the hollow of the belly. This lightens up the dinosaur a little but also allows for more even moisture exchange on both sides of the flanks.

3. Mark out the location for the handle and drill a ⅝-in. hole through the neck. Use a drill press or portable drill stand so the hole is straight, and be sure to back up the cut to avoid tearout when the drill bit exits.

Making the Legs and Flanks

Joining the legs to the flanks

You need to lay out the locations for the legs on the flank pattern—if you didn't do this earlier—and then cut out the area of each leg from the pattern (if you're planning to make more than one dinosaur, you may want to make up another pattern for just this purpose). You then use this leg-location pattern to ensure that the legs go on in the same place on both sides of the animal.

1. Trace the leg locations onto the flanks, making sure you make up a left and a right flank, with the legs on the outside of each (see **Photo D**).

2. Drill pilot holes for the #8 by 2-in. screws that will attach the legs. Drill first from the outside, using the marked locations for the legs as a guide for where to drill. The hind legs get four screws and the forelegs three. Turn the flanks over and countersink for the screw heads. The screws for the forelegs should be countersunk just barely below the surface. Countersink the screws for the hind legs about ¼ in. below the surface.

3. Clamp each leg in place (use clamp pads to protect the surfaces from denting), and insert and tighten the screws from the inside of the flank. Don't use any glue yet; there is still some shaping and smoothing to come.

Joining the flanks to the main body

1. Locate each of the flanks on the main body. The fit will not be perfect, although it should be pretty close.

2. Trace the location of each of the flanks on the body.

3. Clamp one side in place and drill pilot holes through the main body for four #10 by 3-in. screws to attach the flank (see **Photo E**).

4. For the opposite side, you'll have to drill pilot holes for the #8 by 2-in. screws from the outside of the flank. These will be plugged later. Don't use any glue yet; this is only a temporary assembly.

Adding Details and Assembling

Chamfering the edges

Most of the edges on the dinosaur need to be chamfered. But there are some important exceptions; you must avoid the areas where the parts join together (see "Chamfering the Body Parts" on p. 132).

1. Check to be sure that you have accurate pencil marks on the flanks where the legs attach.

2. Mark the insides of the legs where the flanks connect, so you'll know where to stop the chamfers.

3. Now rout the chamfers, but stay out of the sections on the main body, the flanks, and the legs where parts join to each other. Start and stop these chamfers about ½ in. away from the lines. You'll work on the transitions after assembly. Don't chamfer the teeth at all.

Assembling the body

It's finally time to put it all together. Screw and glue all of the body parts together for strength.

1. Attach the legs to the flanks. Apply glue sparingly and keep it at least ½ in. away

PHOTO E: Screw one flank to the main body from inside. The second flank has to be screwed on from the outside.

from the edges of the leg to minimize squeeze-out.

2. Attach one flank, which you can screw into place from the inside of the main body.

3. Attach the opposite flank.

4. Plug the pilot holes, cut off the plugs, and sand flush. You may want to add some wood filler if the plugs do not fill the holes perfectly.

Smoothing again

1. Now you have to go back over the areas where the main body and the flank join

Chamfering the Body Parts

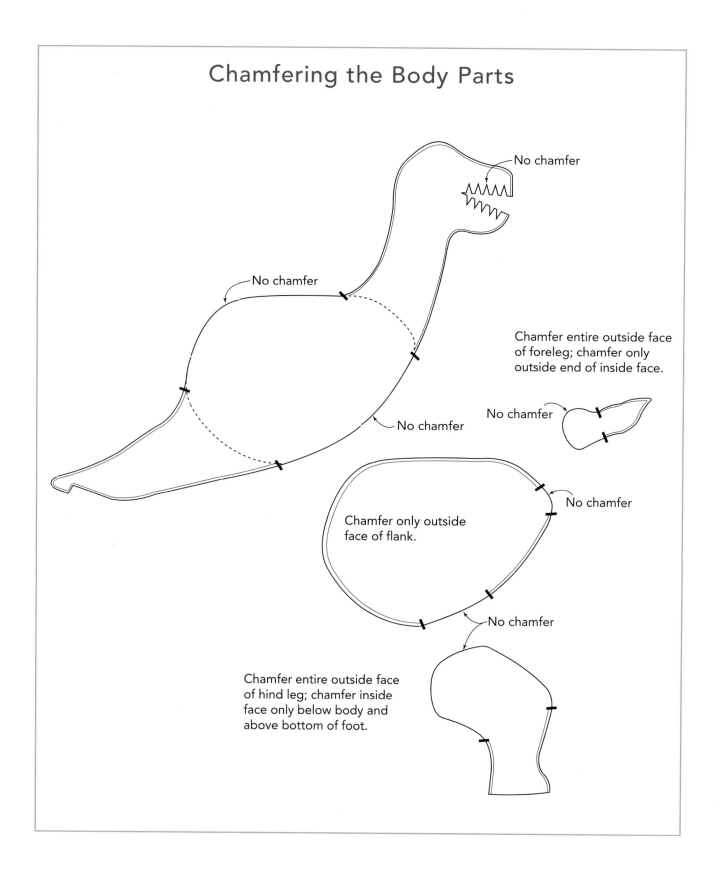

No chamfer

No chamfer

No chamfer

Chamfer entire outside face of foreleg; chamfer only outside end of inside face.

No chamfer

No chamfer

Chamfer only outside face of flank.

No chamfer

Chamfer entire outside face of hind leg; chamfer inside face only below body and above bottom of foot.

together and make these flush and smooth. Use the same tools you used for smoothing the first time around.

2. Work on the transitions at the start of the chamfers, so they grow out of the joint between the body parts.

Making the Rockers

The rockers are strongest if you make them by laminating together thin strips of wood, using a pair of forms. That way, there is almost no chance of the rocker breaking, since there won't be any grain running across the rocker to create a weak spot (short grain). But you can make each rocker from a single piece of solid wood, if you make them about ½ in. thicker than given in the cut list. Either way, the rockers should be made of maple for strength.

Cutting the strips

It is risky to rip on the table saw with the fence set less than 1 in. from the blade. One safe way to saw strips for laminating the rockers is to rip them off a wider board running between the blade and the table-saw fence—the strip being ripped is to the outside of the blade. Unfortunately, this means resetting the fence for every cut.

1. For each rocker, you'll need a 1¾-in.-thick board at least 4 in. wide and roughly 43 in. long. Be sure that there's minimal clearance between the throat plate and the blade, and use a push stick.

2. Assuming your sawblade is ⅛ in. thick, set the rip fence to cut ¼ in. less than the width of the board. This will produce a ⅛-in.-thick strip. Rip a strip.

3. Reset the fence ¼ in. closer to the blade and rip another strip. Continue until you have 11⅛-in.-thick strips or enough to make up a bundle that is 1⅜ in. thick (see "Making the Rocker Forms" on p. 134).

Gluing up the rockers

As with all glue-ups, be prepared and have everything you need close at hand. This is especially true when laminating the rockers.

1. Get together the clamps, glue (I prefer Weldwood plastic-resin glue for laminations), a paint roller with a short-nap roller cover, a tarp to cover the floor and protect it from glue (if necessary) the cauls, and the bundle of strips for one rocker.

2. Spread the strips out on the floor adjacent to one another, keeping one of the strips aside, so you don't spread glue on it.

3. Pour a puddle of glue into the middle of the array of strips and spread it around, using the paint roller. Cover the surface of the strips evenly, adding glue as needed.

4. Stack the strips in order, so there's no glue on the bottom face of the stack. The strip you set aside (the one that has no glue on it) should be last, so there is no glue on the top of the stack, either.

5. Place the stack of glued strips between the rocker forms, and clamp. The first clamp should go roughly in the middle of the forms. Then work your way out to the ends,

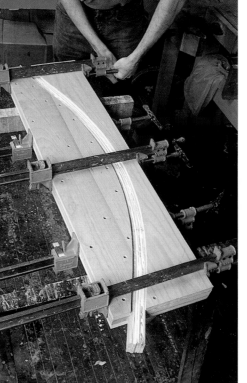

TIP
Wax the rocker forms to keep the glued-up rockers from sticking.

PHOTO F: The clamps should alternate between top and bottom to provide even pressure. You'll need at least five or six heavy-duty clamps.

MAKING THE ROCKER FORMS

The main part of the rockers is based on a 38-in. radius measured at the outside of the rocker. The back 5 in. and front 3 in. flatten out. The lower (concave) form is constructed first and is made up of three layers of ¾-in. plywood. Shape the first layer carefully and then use a flush-trimming bit to cut the subsequent layers. The mating (convex) form must be shaped to allow for 11 strips of maple. Note that the cut-off from the first form is not the right curve.

To draw the correct curve, make a wooden marking disk. Cut it from ¼-in. plywood using an adjustable hole cutter. To use it, slip a pencil point through the hole in the center.

Rolling an appropriate-size wooden disk with a pencil in the center along the concave rocker form marks out the shape needed for the mating form.

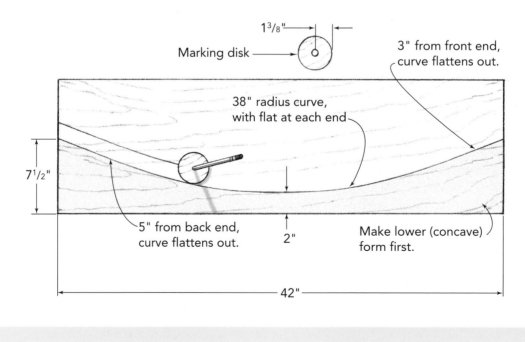

Trace curve of lower (concave) form to mark curve of mating (convex) form, using wooden disk to allow for thickness of 11 laminate strips.

Marking disk → 1³/₈"

3" from front end, curve flattens out.

38" radius curve, with flat at each end

7¹/₂"

5" from back end, curve flattens out.

2"

Make lower (concave) form first.

42"

alternating clamps on the top and the bottom of the assembly (see **Photo F** on p. 133).
6. Let the lamination sit in clamps overnight; then repeat the process for the other rocker.

Smoothing the rockers

Smoothing is a process that is best done with a jointer and planer.

1. Joint one of the edges of the rocker, keeping the bottom of the rocker against the fence. It will probably take a few passes to get through the glue and the unevenness of the layers (see **Photo G**). Note that it is not especially good for the jointer knives to cut through the glue, and you may wind up with small nicks in the knives.

2. Run the rocker through the planer to clean up the opposite edge. Plane down to 1⁹⁄₁₆ in. thick. This should clean up the opposite side completely.

3. Cut the ends to shape on the bandsaw and then sand smooth.

4. Round over the bottom edges of the rockers, routing with ¼-in. roundover bit. Ease the top edges with some sandpaper.

5. Go over everything with sandpaper to smooth out any unevenness.

Making the rocker crosspiece

The crosspiece holds the two rockers together toward the back and provides a way to attach the dinosaur's tail to the rockers.

1. Make up the crosspiece according to the dimensions given in the cut list. While you're at it, cut a piece of scrap plywood to 5¹⁄₁₆ in. by about 10 in. to use as a spacer when attaching the rockers.

2. Drill pilot holes for attaching to the rockers. These should be pocket-screw holes (see "Rocker Crosspiece Details" on p. 136).

Attaching the rockers

1. You may need to reshape the bottoms of the legs slightly to mate with the rockers. Set the dinosaur on the rockers and see if you need to adjust the feet. Sand to fit if necessary. Move the dinosaur forward or back on

PHOTO G: Jointing the edge of the laminated rocker is quick and easy, but it is hard on the jointer knives.

the rockers until the back of the leg is closest to the floor when the rockers come to rest from rocking. Mark the position of the legs on the rockers.

2. Hold the dinosaur upside down in a bench vise. Clamp the 5¹⁄₁₆-in.-wide spacer between the rockers, making sure that the ends of the rockers line up. Place the clamped-up rocker assembly upside down

TIP

Use a carbide scraper to remove as much glue as possible before running a glue-up through a planer or over a jointer.

Rocker Crosspiece Details

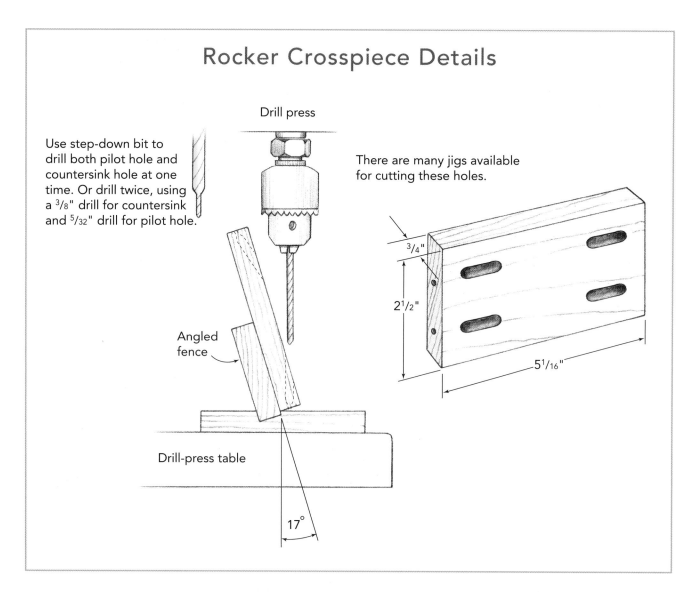

Use step-down bit to drill both pilot hole and countersink hole at one time. Or drill twice, using a 3/8" drill for countersink and 5/32" drill for pilot hole.

Drill press

There are many jigs available for cutting these holes.

Angled fence

Drill-press table

17°

3/4"

2 1/2"

5 1/16"

PHOTO H: Clamp a spacer block the same width as the rocker crosspiece between the rockers, making sure the rocker ends line up. With the dinosaur mounted upside down in the bench vise, position the rocker assembly; then drill pilot holes and screw the rockers to the legs.

on the inverted dinosaur, using the alignment mark made in Step 1 (see **Photo H**).

3. Drill pilot holes for two screws in each leg and two through the crosspiece into the tail. The two pilot holes for the legs should angle in toward one another.

4. Attach the rockers to the legs with #10 by 3-in. screws. Plug the holes and sand flush.

5. Screw the rocker crosspiece to the tail with two #6 by 1¼-in. screws.

6. Screw the crosspiece to the rockers with #6 by 1¼-in. screws (see **Photo I**).

Creating the Final Touches

1. Insert an 8½-in.-long by ⅝-in. dowel into the hole in the neck of the dinosaur. Center the dowel.

2. Drill a pilot hole for a #6 by 1¼-in. screw in from the front of the neck and through the dowel (see **Photo J**).

3. Insert the screw to pin the dowel in place. Then plug the hole. When the glue has dried, cut the plug off and sand flush.

Finishing

Paint the dinosaur with a nontoxic paint. The color scheme is up to you. One current theory holds that dinosaurs were brightly colored. Why not?

Go ahead and give it a little test ride!

PHOTO I: Screw the crosspiece in place after attaching it to the tail.

PHOTO J: Aim your drill toward the handle; then drill and screw to lock the handle in place.

TOY CHEST

A TOY CHEST IS SOMETHING different for a grown-up than it is for a child. For the child it's simply a place to stash everything when told to put stuff away. It needs to be big. Once in a while, it's also a place to play; either on or in. It should be fun. For a grown-up it represents all that, plus a preserve for orderliness or at least a place to hide the mess. But first and foremost it has to be safe. The lid must be well supported so it can't slam on fingers, and it must not close air-tight, in case someone does decide to play inside of it.

This toy chest fills the requirements for both. It's also fairly easy to build, being relatively free of complicated woodworking joints. It can be made of a hardwood or edge-banded plywood, nicely finished, or poplar or soft maple that is painted and decorated. There's an optional inner tray to help organize some of the junk inside. For safety, there is a lid stay (support)—not at all optional—to prevent the lid from slamming. The front edge of the box is lowered to protect fingers further and to provide ventilation in case a child closes himself or herself inside.

TOY CHEST

THE FIVE PANELS THAT MAKE up the box of the toy chest are screwed together, making for simple joinery. The ball feet are purchased but are modified using a special jig. The molding that runs around the box adds character to it all and is easy to make with a drill press.

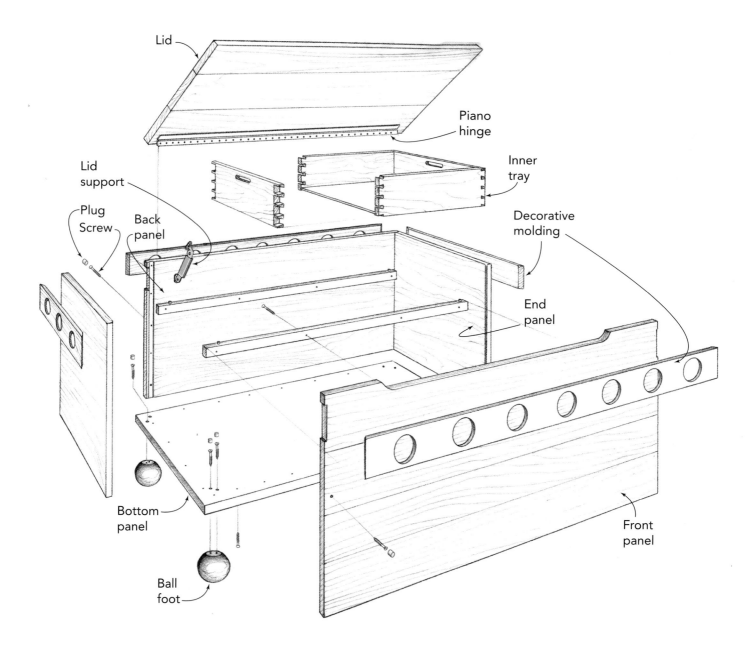

Lid

Piano hinge

Inner tray

Lid support

Plug Screw

Back panel

Decorative molding

End panel

Bottom panel

Ball foot

Front panel

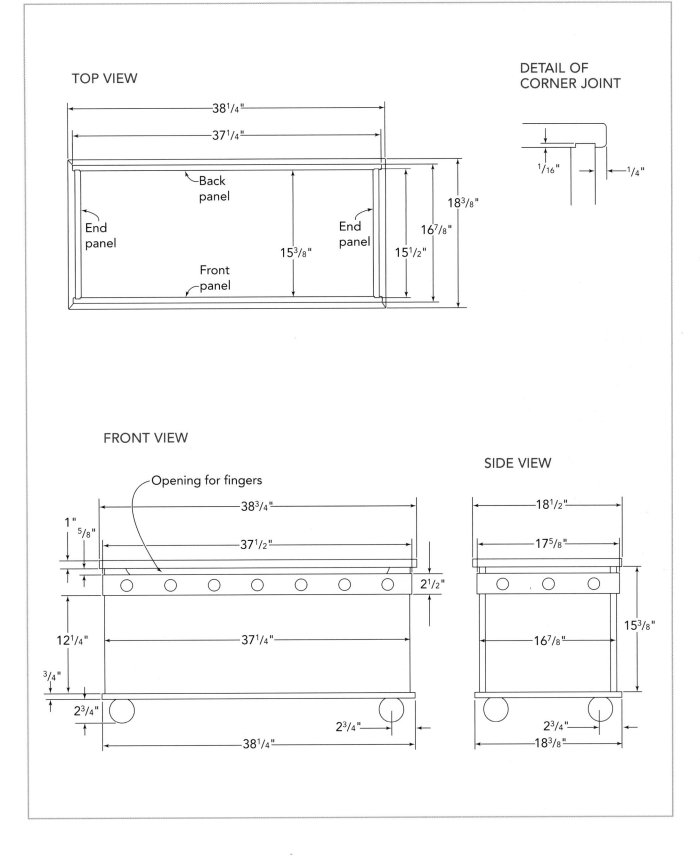

TOP VIEW

38$\frac{1}{4}$"

37$\frac{1}{4}$"

Back panel

End panel

End panel

Front panel

15$\frac{3}{8}$"

15$\frac{1}{2}$"

16$\frac{7}{8}$"

18$\frac{3}{8}$"

DETAIL OF CORNER JOINT

$\frac{1}{16}$"

$\frac{1}{4}$"

FRONT VIEW

Opening for fingers

1"

$\frac{5}{8}$"

38$\frac{3}{4}$"

37$\frac{1}{2}$"

2$\frac{1}{2}$"

12$\frac{1}{4}$"

37$\frac{1}{4}$"

$\frac{3}{4}$"

2$\frac{3}{4}$"

2$\frac{3}{4}$"

38$\frac{1}{4}$"

SIDE VIEW

18$\frac{1}{2}$"

17$\frac{5}{8}$"

16$\frac{7}{8}$"

15$\frac{3}{8}$"

2$\frac{3}{4}$"

18$\frac{3}{8}$"

CUT LIST FOR TOY CHEST

2	Panels (1 front and 1 back)	¾" x 15⅜" x 37¼"
2	End panels	¾" x 15⅜" x 15½"
1	Bottom panel	¾" x 15½" x 35½"*
2	Edge pieces	¾" x 1⅜" x 38¼" (cut to fit)
2	Edge pieces	¾" x 1⅜" x 18¼" (cut to fit)
4	Wooden balls	3" dia.
1	Top	1" x 18½" x 38¾"
2	Decorative molding pieces	⅜" x 2½" x 17½"
2	Decorative molding pieces	⅜" x 2½" x 37½"
Hardware		
	Screws	#6 x 1⅝"
	Screws	#6 x 2"
	Wooden plugs	
1	Piano hinge	1½" x 36" (cut down to 34")
1	Lid stay	
Optional Inner Tray		
2	Sides	½" x 4½" x 15"
2	Ends	½" x 4½" x 15¼"
1	Bottom	¼" plywood, 14½" x 14¾"
2	Cleats	¾" x 1" x 35¼"
4	Screw-on rubber bumpers	⅝" dia.

*Hardwood plywood.

Three-Quarter View

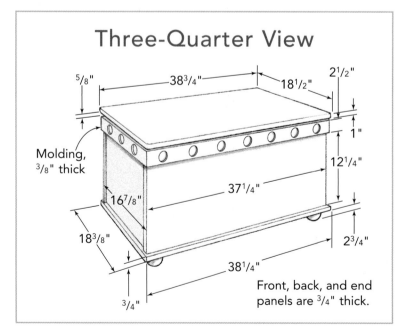

5/8" 38³/4" 18¹/2" 2¹/2"

Molding, 3/8" thick

1"

12¹/4"

37¹/4"

16⁷/8"

18³/8"

2³/4"

38¹/4"

3/4"

Front, back, and end panels are 3/4" thick.

THERE ARE LOTS OF WAYS to put together the four sides of a box like this. I opted for the relative simplicity of dadoes and screws, because I didn't really want to see a lot of joinery at the corners.

Making the Box

Preparing the panels

Start by preparing all of the panels that will make up the box.

1. Mill all of the wood for the chest front, back, and sides to ¾ in. thick. If you're making a chest of a nice hardwood, you might rip all of this stock to the same width or along lines that yield the best of the wood's figure.

2. Mill the wood for the top to 1 in. thick.

3. Joint all edges straight and smooth.

4. Arrange the boards the way you want them and mark them with a layout triangle so you can put them back together in order.

5. Check the edges to be sure they are all straight. If not, rejoint and check again.

6. Get everything you'll need for a glue-up; then glue the boards together. Leave the boards in clamps for at least 1 hour or 2 hours if you're using yellow glue. Don't move on to smoothing out the panels for at least 24 hours.

7. Plane, scrape, and/or sand the panels flat and smooth.

8. Cut the panels to size.

9. Round over the ends of the front and back panels slightly. I used a 1/8-in. round-over bit in the router.

Cutting the box joinery

It doesn't really matter how you put the boards together, as long as the basic box is secure. I dadoed the front and back panels, rabbeted the sides to fit, and then screwed the box together (see "Joinery Details").

1. Cut a ¹⁄₁₆-in.-deep by ⅝-in.-wide dado on the inside face of both ends of the front and back panels, ¼ in. away from the edges (see **Photo A**).

2. Cut a shallow rabbet on the inside of each end of the end panels; then fit the end panels into the dadoes in the front and rear panels.

3. Drill four countersunk pilot holes for #6 by 1⅝-in. screws in the front and rear panels so the screws will be centered on the end panels; these should be ¹¹⁄₁₆ in. from the ends of the front and back panels.

4. Lay out and then cut the notches for the decorative molding ⅝ in. down from the top edge of both the front and the back panels (see "Joinery Details"). These notches should be 2½ in. wide (exactly the same as the molding) and at least deep enough to reach the dado for the end panels. Because it is not critical that the bottoms of the notches be

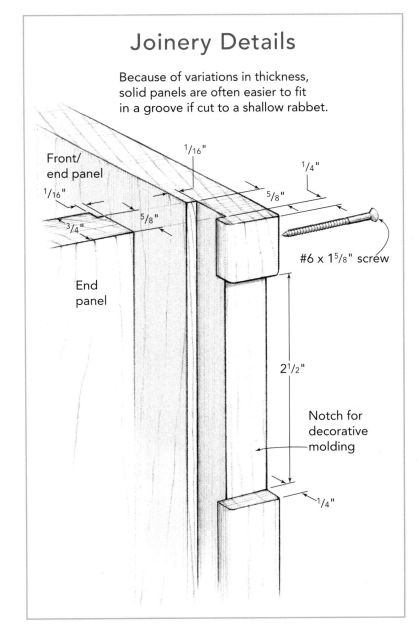

Joinery Details

Because of variations in thickness, solid panels are often easier to fit in a groove if cut to a shallow rabbet.

Front/end panel

1/16"

1/16"

3/4"

5/8"

5/8"

1/4"

#6 x 1⅝" screw

End panel

2½"

Notch for decorative molding

1/4"

PHOTO A: Cut the dadoes on the front and rear panels on the table saw. A crosscut sled makes the job safer and easier.

PHOTO B: I cut the notches for the decorative molding on the bandsaw. After cutting both ends of the notch, I nibbled away enough wood to leave room for the blade and then I cut along the bottom of the notch.

PHOTO C: You can use the hinge itself as an accurate positioning jig for drilling the pilot holes for the screws. A self-centering drill bit makes the job much easier.

perfectly smooth, I just cut out the notches on the bandsaw, which required no special setup (see **Photo B**).

Assembling the box

1. Spread a small amount of glue into each of the dadoes.
2. Fit the panels into position, aligning the top and bottom edges and holding them together with clamps. Then drive the screws into the pilot holes.
3. Plug the holes.

Sanding the outside and leveling the edges

1. When the glue is dry, cut off the plugs and sand them flush with the panel surface.
2. Go over the rest of the box and sand where necessary. Be sure to sand the end grain on the front and rear panels.
3. Level off the top and bottom edges by planing or sanding carefully with a sanding block. On the bottom, the goal is a flat edge that will mate well with the bottom of the toy chest. The top back and side edges should be eased enough so they will not cause any scrapes or scratches. Don't worry about the front edge for now.

Locating the lid hinge

Because the decorative molding will get in the way of setting up the piano hinge on the back of the box, this is a good time to drill the pilot holes for all of the screws.
1. Cut the piano hinge to 34 in. long or close to that length while cutting at a seam. File the cut edges smooth.
2. Open the piano hinge as far as it will go (this should be roughly 270 degrees), and place it on the back edge of the chest with the knuckle up and to the outside and with the unfolded leaf extending down outside of the back. This unfolded leaf will work as a stop to hold the hinge in the right position (see **Photo C**).
3. Drill the pilot holes for the screws. This is easy to do with a self-centering drill bit.
4. Set aside the hinge and the screws for later.

Making the decorative molding

The molding has no function, but it is one of the things that makes the overall design work.
1. Mill the stock for the molding to ⅜ in. thick and rip to width. It's a good idea to sand the outside face now as well, before you start drilling the holes in it.
2. Cut the strips roughly to length (a couple inches long is fine for now). Miter one end of each strip.
3. Fit each piece to the case and mark out the opposite end. It may help to have a

mitered piece of scrap to hold around the corner, so you're sure that the end is in exactly the right place before marking the end you need to cut. Cut each of the strips to length.

4. Lay out the locations for the holes (see "Decorative Molding ").

5. Drill the holes, then ease all of the outside edges.

6. Attach the molding to the box by gluing and clamping in place. Be careful with the glue, so you don't have to clean up a lot of squeeze-out inside the holes.

Making the Base of the Chest

Begin work on the bottom of the toy chest by cutting a piece of hardwood plywood to about ⅛ in. less than the outer dimensions of your box. This way, the seam for the solid-wood edge-banding will remain covered.

Edging the bottom of the chest

1. Mill the wood for the edge pieces to ¾ in. thick (about 1⁄32 in. thicker than the plywood) and rip to 1⅜ in. wide. Cut into pieces long enough for each edge (including the miters on the ends).

2. Miter one end of each of the edge pieces.

3. Scribe the location of the opposite corner onto the inside of the edge pieces (see **Photo D**).

4. Cut the miter on this corner so it just touches your scribed line. Note that the two pieces may be slightly different if your plywood is not exactly square. Mark carefully so you know which piece goes on which side.

5. Glue the two longer pieces of edging to the plywood bottom.

6. When the glue is dry, remove the clamps and work on getting the short edge pieces to fit. Mark carefully, then cut to size. I like to start long and work slowly toward a perfect fit. Repeat for the other end.

7. Glue the end pieces on. Spread some glue on the miters as well as on the edges, and clamp in place.

8. Plane and sand the edging flush with the panels. It's best not to plane through

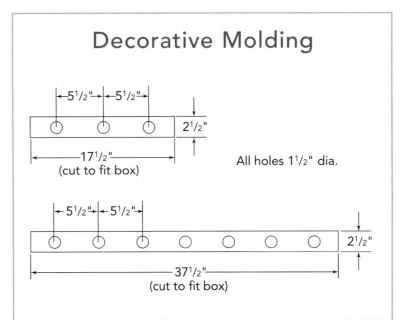

Decorative Molding

All holes 1½" dia.

PHOTO D: Accuracy when cutting the mitered edge pieces comes from working methodically and checking each piece in its place.

the veneer on the panel, but don't worry about it too much, since the seam is hidden from view.

9. Sand the edges smooth. Then round over both the top and bottom edges on all four sides with a ¼-in. roundover bit in a router.

Making the ball feet

The feet are 3-in.-diameter round balls that are commercially available in maple (see

Jig for Ball Feet

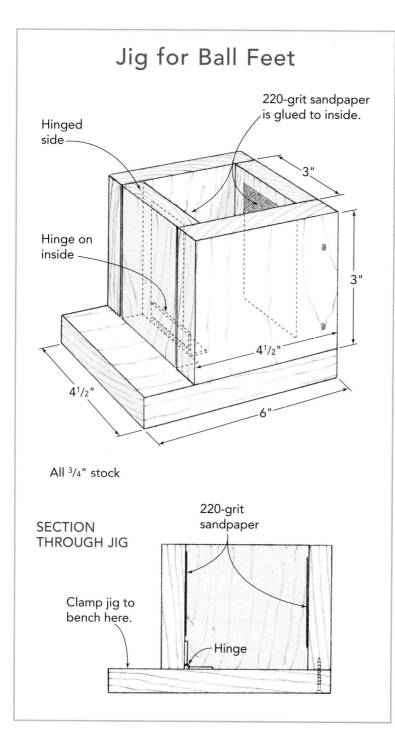

Hinged side

Hinge on inside

220-grit sandpaper is glued to inside.

3"

3"

4½"

4½"

6"

All ¾" stock

SECTION THROUGH JIG

220-grit sandpaper

Clamp jig to bench here.

Hinge

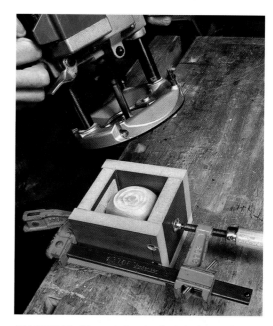

PHOTO E: Clamp the ball tightly in the jig and the jig securely to the bench. Then rout the flat on the top with a straight bit.

2. While the ball is still in the jig, mark out a spot roughly in the center of the flat; then drill a ³⁄₃₂-in. pilot hole about 1½ in. deep for the screw that will attach the ball to the bottom of the chest.

Attaching the feet to the bottom

Attach the feet to the bottom of the chest with screws and glue.

1. Mark out the location for each of the feet on the top of the bottom panel, at a point 2¾ in. from each of the edges. Mark the upper face of the bottom panel.

2. Drill countersunk pilot holes down from the top of the bottom panel on your marks.

3. Put a daub of glue on the flat on the top of the foot, then insert a #6 by 2-in. screw in the pilot hole closest to the corner in the bottom panel until it just sticks out the underside. Place a foot in place and screw down tight (see **Photo F**). Add the second screw. Repeat for each of the other feet.

4. Plug the countersunk holes; then cut off the plugs and sand them flush with the surface of the bottom panel.

"Sources" on p. 151). You can turn your own ball feet, if you'd like.

1. You need to cut a flat on the top of each of the balls. Removing about ¼ in. will leave a flat that is roughly 1½ in. in diameter. For this, you need to make a jig to hold the ball securely during the work (see **Photo E** and "Jig for Ball Feet").

PHOTO F: Hold the ball foot to keep it from turning when you tighten the screw.

Attaching the bottom to the chest

1. Mark out and drill countersunk pilot holes for the screws to attach the bottom to the box. There should be three evenly spaced holes on each end and five evenly spaced holes on each side. Be sure to drill and countersink from the underside of the bottom panel.

2. Place the box upside down on a pair of sawhorses or a workbench and position the bottom panel carefully. When the panel is centered on the box, clamp in place and secure with #6 by 1⅝-in. screws.

3. Plug all of the holes; then trim off with a chisel or saw and sand the plugs flush with the bottom.

Making the Lid

The lid is 2 in. longer but only 1⅜ in. wider than the box (the back can't overhang as much as the sides or front).

1. Cut the lid to size (see "Lid Details").

2. Smooth all of the edges and use a ⅜-in.-radius router bit to round over all but the back underside edge where the hinge will go.

3. A solid-wood top on an enclosed box like this would usually be subject to some warping, since the moisture content of the air outside a closed box can be different from that on the inside. The ventilation slot and the fact that the lid does not sit completely tight to the box help equalize things here. If

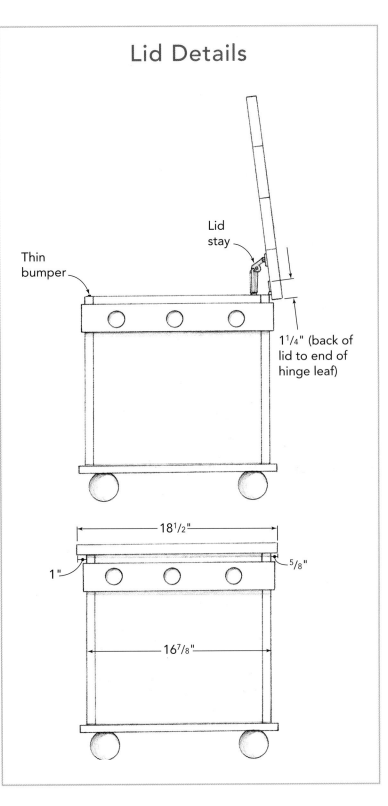

Lid Details

Thin bumper

Lid stay

1¼" (back of lid to end of hinge leaf)

18½"

1"

⅝"

16⅞"

you have problems with warping, you can add battens to the underside of the lid. The outer holes for screwing the battens to the lid must be elongated to allow for wood movement; the center holes do not need this.

PHOTO G: The bearing of the flush-trimming bit references off the edge of the decorative molding. The cut is stopped when the router base contacts the box.

PHOTO H: Mark the hinge location on the underside of the lid after centering the lid on the chest.

Routing the front top edge of the box

The top edge of the front of the box is recessed to keep fingers from getting smashed there when the lid is closed and to provide ventilation in case someone decides to play inside the box.

1. Tip the box forward onto the front face.

2. Using a router with a flush-trimming bit, rout the top of the front panel flush with the decorative molding. You may want to clamp a piece of scrap into place on the right side of the box to prevent the router from chipping out some of the edge as it exits the cut (see **Photo G**).

3. Sand the routed edge smooth and ease the corners.

Hinging the lid

The lid can overhang the back of the box by only ⅝ in.; any longer and it will bang into the molding on the back. The lid will not be able to open more than 90 degrees because of the lid stay, so the overhang, which would otherwise keep it from opening more than that, won't be a problem.

1. Place the hinge on the back edge of the box and drive in a few screws to hold it in position. Close the hinge. Place the top on the box, positioning it so that it's centered from side to side and the back edge is flush with the outside of the box. Mark out the ends of the hinge on the underside of the top (see **Photo H**). Remove the lid, and unscrew and remove the hinge.

2. Transfer your end marks forward 1 in.; then scribe a line 1¼ in. from the back edge of the lid.

3. Clamp the hinge in position with the edge of the leaf on the scribed line and the ends lined up with the end marks.

4. Drill pilot holes for the screws.

5. Screw the hinge to the box. Then hold the lid in place and screw the other leaf of the hinge to the lid.

Adding the lid stay

It is critical that you add a lid stay to support the lid in any position so it can't drop down on fingers. Lid stays generally come with specific mounting instructions. The lid stay I used has a strong spring and a cam. It is very effective.

Finishing

However you decide to finish the outside of the toy chest, don't use an oil finish on the inside. This will smell rancid after just a short time. I used an oil-and-wax finish on the outside and shellac on the inside.

THE OPTIONAL INNER TRAY

Make the optional inner tray about 15 in. long and 1/8 in. less in length than the inside distance between the front and the back. I made the tray 4½ in. high, which left room to rout handles on the ends. The tray sides should be ½ in. thick. Join the tray together however you please, as long as it will be sturdy enough to stand up to some abuse.

Installing the Cleats

Screw the cleats that will support the inner tray into place 5½ in. down from the top. Attach screw-on rubber bumpers to the cleats on both sides. These will keep the tray from banging into the sides of the box and will leave room for the lid stay to fold down. If the lid stay needs more room, move the bumper on that side farther away from the end panel.

This peek inside the toy chest shows the optional inner tray, the cleats it rests on, the rubber bumpers, and the lid support.

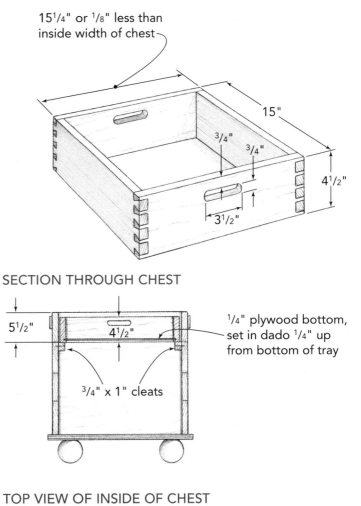

INNER TRAY

15 1/4" or 1/8" less than inside width of chest

15"

3/4"

3/4"

4 1/2"

3 1/2"

SECTION THROUGH CHEST

5 1/2"

4 1/2"

1/4" plywood bottom, set in dado 1/4" up from bottom of tray

3/4" x 1" cleats

TOP VIEW OF INSIDE OF CHEST

Rubber bumper

Lid stay

Rubber bumper

Back panel

Cleat

1/2"

1 1/2"

End panel

1 1/2"

Cleat

1/2"

Rubber bumper

Front panel

Rubber bumper

SOURCES

Although most of the supplies needed for the projects in this book can be found at a decent hardware or "big box" store, there are some things you might have to look for elsewhere. The following are just a few of the places I've turned to for supplies.

AURO USA
1340-G Industrial Ave.
Petaluma, CA 94952
(888) 302-9352
www.aurousa.com
Natural plant-based paints and finishes

CONSTANTINES
2050 Eastchester Rd.
Bronx, NY 10461
(800) 223-8087
www.constantines.com
Tools, specialty hardware, and veneers, including checkerboard assemblies

FLAMINGO
Flamingo Specialty
Veneer Company Inc.
356 Glenwood Ave.
East Orange, NJ 07017
(973) 672-7600
(973) 675-7778 FAX
Veneer and veneering supplies

GARRETT WADE
161 Avenue of the Americas
New York, NY 10013
(800) 221-2942
Woodworking tools and supplies

HIGHLAND HARDWARE
1045 N. Highland Ave. NE
Atlanta, GA 30306
(800) 241-6748
Tools, woodworking supplies, and finishes

LEE VALLEY
P.O. Box 1780
Ogdensburg, NY 13669
(800) 871-8158
Cupboard locks, knife hinges, hardware, tools, and woodworking supplies

LIE-NIELSEN TOOLWORKS
P.O. Box 9, Route 1
Warren, ME 04864
(800) 327-2520
Exceptional handplanes

LIVOS PHYTOCHEMISTRY
OF AMERICA, INC.
P.O. Box 1740
Mashpee, MA 02649
(508) 477-7955
www.livos.com
All-natural, plant-based oils and waxes

MIDWEST DOWEL WORKS
4631 Hutchinson Rd.
Cincinnati, OH 45248
(800) 555-0133
Dowels in a variety of sizes and woods

ROCKLER
4365 Willow Dr.
Medina, MN 55340
(800) 279-4441
All sorts of hardware (including connector bolts and cap nuts) and finish supplies (including flake shellac)

WOODCRAFT
P.O. Box 1686
560 Airport Industrial Rd.
Parkersburg, WV 26102
(800) 225-1153
Hinges, locks, box feet, hardware, tools, and woodworking supplies

WOODWORKER'S HARDWARE
P.O. Box 180
Sauk Rapids, MN 56379
(800) 383-0130
Drawer slides, hanging file rails, casters, hinges, clothes rods, locks, catches, pulls, etc.

WOODWORKER'S SUPPLY
1108 N. Glen Rd.
Casper, WY 82601
(800) 645-9292
Large dowels, General Finishes Seal-A-Cell and Arm-R-Seal, hardware, tools, and woodworking supplies

METRIC CONVERSION CHART

Inches	Centimeters	Millimeters	Inches	Centimeters	Millimeters
1/8	0.3	3	13	33.0	330
1/4	0.6	6	14	35.6	356
3/8	1.0	10	15	38.1	381
1/2	1.3	13	16	40.6	406
5/8	1.6	16	17	43.2	432
3/4	1.9	19	18	45.7	457
7/8	2.2	22	19	48.3	483
1	2.5	25	20	50.8	508
1 1/4	3.2	32	21	53.3	533
1 1/2	3.8	38	22	55.9	559
1 3/4	4.4	44	23	58.4	584
2	5.1	51	24	61.0	610
2 1/2	6.4	64	25	63.5	635
3	7.6	76	26	66.0	660
3 1/2	8.9	89	27	68.6	686
4	10.2	102	28	71.1	711
4 1/2	11.4	114	29	73.7	737
5	12.7	127	30	76.2	762
6	15.2	152	31	78.7	787
7	17.8	178	32	81.3	813
8	20.3	203	33	83.8	838
9	22.9	229	34	86.4	864
10	25.4	254	35	88.9	889
11	27.9	279	36	91.4	914
12	30.5	305			

OTHER TAUNTON PROJECT BOOKS

HOME STORAGE PROJECTS

Paul Anthony

ISBN 1-56158-498-3

Product #070610

176 pages

BOOKCASES

Niall Barrett

ISBN 1-56158-303-0

Product #070431

192 pages

BUILDING THE CUSTOM HOME OFFICE

Niall Barrett

ISBN 1-56158-421-5

Product #070587

160 pages

CLASSIC KITCHEN PROJECTS

Niall Barrett

ISBN 1-56158-386-3

Product #070512

176 pages

DESKS

Andy Charron

ISBN 1-56158-348-0

Product #070489

160 pages

DINING TABLES

Kim Carleton Graves with Masha Zager

ISBN 1-56158-491-6

Product #070609

192 pages

TABLES

Anthony Guidice

ISBN 1-56158-342-1

Product #070469

176 pages

CHESTS OF DRAWERS

Bill Hylton

ISBN 1-56158-422-3

Product #070618

224 pages

BEDS

Jeff Miller

ISBN 1-56158-254-9

Product #070379

192 pages